I0664790

Read This Please Volume One

Editions 1 - 6

Edited by Sheila Cano and Donna Lewis

Contributing Writers: *Steven Bird, Sheila Cano, B G Lewis, Adrienne S Moody, Thomas Pryce, Bruce Reisner, Casimirr Rexregys, Sarah Scott, M Dawn Thacker, Trularin, and Gaboo. Special thanks to Steve Bryson and Donna Lewis for their technical and organizational skills making this happen.*

sage
press

Vancouver, Canada

Read This Please
Volume One / 2011
Copyright © 2011 ReadThisPlease.com

Published by Sage Press, Vancouver, Canada

Read This Please Volume One / ReadThisPlease.com

ISBN: 978-0-9809201-6-1

Literary Collections/General. Format: Paperback book, text
Release: 20110801

Cover art: ReadThisPlease.com
Contact: info@readthisplease.com or order online at
Now.readthisplease.com

Read This Please

Volume One

Table of Contents

Volume 1 Edition 3 – Father, Where art thou?

Volume 1 Edition 4 - Harvest Edition

Volume 1 Edition 5 - Stop, you're scaring me! 257

Read This Please

Volume 1 Edition 1 - Places & Spaces

March 15, 2010

Welcome to the first edition of our online magazine. This compilation begins way back, when we first thought to release stories as a group. ReadThisPlease.com invites you to travel with us on a theme of 'Places & Spaces'.

Clearing My Head
by Sarah Scott

Morning breaks and light bursts forth into the world, but you are filled with darkness, creeping along in the shadows, pounding on walls, with no feeling, isolated, jaded forever.

It's a cycle, you tell yourself. It will end in a week, or maybe two, but what if it never does? What if you never slither back to civilization? You must. You must creep back to that peaceful place, pull yourself into the light. Let it burn holes through the ice facade surrounding you. Your survival depends upon it. Do not sink forever into the night—fight. Battle the demons tormenting you and break the chains imprisoning your soul. Find freedom. Find peace.

And when you find your way back home, my loving arms will be waiting. I want to help you, but I cannot follow to the place you've gone. I'm not that strong. Come back to me, sweet peace of mind. I'm waiting here for you to win the fight. Defeat the night.

Doing Time in Nursery School
by Sheila Cano

I remember going to nursery school when I was about four years old. I'm not sure exactly where it was in the city, but it was an old building with a bronze fountain out front, and a fence along the street made of iron spears. The cherub boy atop the fountain urinated perpetually into a concrete basin.

Indoors, the space was large with high ceilings, paneled dark woodwork, and shiny wooden floors. Sounds echoed inside what was probably a gymnasium, part of a school. We listened to stories of *Pippi Longstocking,* and *The Little Engine That Could*. The storyteller showed us pictures in the book. We played games with beanbags and balls, arranged large wooden blocks, and snacked on apple juice and graham crackers. Then we were supposed to take a nap, lying on floor mats, covered with light blankets. I could not sleep, and lay looking up at the dark wooden ceiling with lights hanging high overhead, glaring down on me.

I was frustrated at being inside this dark building, listening to stories instead of being able to hold the book and read it myself. I didn't like the routines laid out for us, though I did enjoy the

9

snack. I don't remember how long I went there, perhaps a couple of weeks. One day, Mom asked me how I liked nursery school. According to her, I answered, "How would you like to be locked up all day?"

No Needles

by B G Lewis

The dentist's office hosts a symphony—an opera—and the string section is exquisite. Their performance is the highlight of any visit. Vibrant, pulsating notes climb effortlessly from silicon and Swedish steel. A whirling crescendo dances on enamel fret boards, springing into a chorus in the lobby of the third floor dental center.

The staff are cheerful players. Overly cheerful. It's in the center's marketing strategy. Pastel hygienists direct patients on and off the stage. The only staid performance comes from the receptionist, singly ushering reluctant appointments onto her computer screen. However, her mastery of the incoming call is flawless. A tone chimes once and she answers. A moment's pause and the tone chimes again and she answers. This halting measure repeats again, and again. The meter is riveting.

Patrons of the dentist sit politely, quietly and await their own private recital. A child discovers the nook of toys and a bounty of color and plastic amusement. All perfectly generic and safe props on the set: rollers and bouncers, figurines and blocks, each smeared in snot and earwax. They're not much different than the

11

toys at home, but they're fresh and they're here, and it's okay to build a world for twenty minutes while your sister is offstage in a big chair. The smaller, strange kid joins in and banter perks up.

"Do it this way."

"Lemme see."

"You be this guy."

"This goes this way."

"I got one of these at home!"

Mom wanders, waiting in a dog-eared monthly, her intermission from the players. Lackadaisical, she drifts for a few found, mindless minutes. Her fingers pirouette—flip. A glance—flip. Musing—flip. What does she look at? A face. An outfit. A place? There's a pause, and she hovers in a recipe photo. Tonight—after the show? Too much work.

All the while, the string section is reaching a climax. A high sharp sings alone, spinning, wavering, in solitary aria. The soprano pines and solos, when suddenly another briefly joins in. They sing above all else—an interwoven twine of pitches—perfuming the lobby in burnt aromas of dentin and enamel. When chance synchronizes their duet, it is luscious.

"Payne?"

"Yes."

"Hi I'm Deb—I'll be your hygienist. We're all set in Room Three."

"Great."

Deb is lavender and plump, perpetually smiles, and doubtless the center's star for flowing a tearful five-year-old to a seat. There's a friendly march to her stage movement that begs following. Cheerful Deb.

She leads behind the curtain, past a lit portal of raw drama in Theater One. Slacks and shoes jut from beneath a smock overlaid in pneumatic instruments. Two technical stylists are intent on the gaping, pink maw lying open before them.

Next theater, jeans and runners are in repose, ankles crossed. Rubber dam speak garbles to the delicate notes of saliva babbling in a suction tube. Whisked past in brisk Deb style, Number Three appears at the end of the corridor. Here is an array of fine stainless steel, a crafted selection of refined implements, and a beautiful, full length spectator's chair that beholds center stage. Front row.

"So Payne, you've been to see Dr. Serns before—August tenth?" Deb flips pages through the script.

"That's right."

13

"Okay, so we've got just a bit of drilling today and then Dr. Serns is going to do one filling."

Deb leans forward and attaches splatter attire—an indication that the maestro is near. Her breasts are too large. She is forced to work around them, but compensates well and whirls with velocity. Warmth emanates from her movements.

"Would you like the headphones?"

"No, that's alright. I'm fine."

"A magazine?"

"Everything's perfect."

"OK, I'll be right back. Just relax for a couple minutes and then we'll get you prepped."

Waiting for the conductor's arrival is a happenstance in self reflection, and anticipation. The proscenium seating yaws back and upward, thrusting those in attendance directly into exposure for what will come. The impatient will find the first objects to scrutinize are one's own shoes. Footwear is forefront; wear something fashionable. They're eye level and in a new context. The shoes look back and confide, "This will be an especially vulnerable arrangement."

14

Stage Three is in the corner of the facility, brighter than the others, with large kitty corner windows and a low counter apron. Street level is beyond any sight line from the chair. Innocent pedestrians walk the boulevard below, oblivious to the intensity above; a new opera unfolds twice an hour. The professional marquee and potted junipers lounge in a water feature at the complex entrance, disguising any threat of a bad performance, beckoning with serenity. Such venues would be better appreciated at ground level. Wide, expansive windows would make for better public scrutiny and entertainment. Friends could come to watch friends. Strangers could clamor against viewing glass to witness an intricate root canal or a colorful wisdom tooth extraction. Incredible entertainment value for the curious.

Eventually, the overhead lamp becomes a focal point. It is a stark, face-to-face onlooker to all cues. It stares in dull beige and amber that is never bright enough. The illuminated aid barely has the intensity to hold imagination as it cranes forward. Still, this is an integral player in the opera. The lamp guides and focuses the audience's attention. The lamp is a corner piece of the experience. Refuse shaded eye wear if asked.

"I'm back."

Deb enters from the wings; her welded smile is now costumed in a powder blue mask. "If you can open wide, I'm just going to dab on a bit of topical. Then Dr. Serns will give you some freezing." Deb maneuvers the pastel breasts closer to compensate for arm length.

"No needles."

Deb hesitates in mid benzine application. "Don't worry, Payne. This works really good. It will just numb the area a bit so you won't feel the needle at all."

"I'd prefer not."

"I understand. We have a few patients that are sensitive. I promise you, it goes really quick—you won't feel a thing." Deb's reluctant to give up her stance. That would mean maneuvering back into swabbing position and a slight diminuendo.

"I don't think you understand, Deb. Would you like to take a first class trip to Paris and then have dinner on the plane and fly back—never getting off the runway? I've payed for premier seating and I want to enjoy the experience. No needles, please."

Deb's brow reveals a character not often perplexed. Now the singalong approach that entertains a shy five-year-old is muted.

"You don't want any freezing? Payne, that nerve will be pretty sensitive. Are you sure. No freezing? At all?"

16

"No, thank you."

"O—OK. No freezing."

"Thanks Deb."

Dr. Serns enters the stage. Here is the magnificent cheironomist who will astound the audience with his precision. He is goggled and masked, yet his eyes peer through, reassuring. The virtuoso exudes confidence tantamount in a performance.

"How are you, Payne?" His Latvian accent rolls through his mask in warm tones.

"Excellent, Dr. Serns, it's good to see you."

"Payne doesn't want any freezing," Deb chimes in, transforming from choir leader, and tattling to the principal.

"That's right, I remember." Serns motions and the lamp is closer. He begins his inspection, audience held waiting upon the thrust.

"Payne prefers to experience my wonderful talents live and up front. A real patron of the art," Serns chuckles.

Deb's cheery visage turns to apprehension.

17

"Alright then, Debra," Serns taps upon the tender, white starlet now in the spotlight, "let's start with a M3 on the lower bicuspid. Ready, Payne? Open wide—aah, yes. That's it."

The dentist's office hosts a symphony—an opera. Vibrant notes climb effortlessly from silicon and Swedish steel. A soprano begins its exquisite flight, whirling, dancing on enamel and soaring into aria.

The Parking Lot
by M Dawn Thacker

The woman is running across the parking lot toward me. I am standing there with the Administrator of the nursing home discussing some spring landscaping possibilities with a month's worth of snow piled around us. The woman looks harried, her gray hair blowing back from her face. She is past middle age—and she's at full sprint.

"You work here don't you?" she asks as she runs to within inches of my face.

"Yes I do," I respond. "Are you alright?"

"This parking lot is atrocious, simply awful. I am going to call your company. There's just no excuse for it," she says, her breath rasping from her. I look at her with confusion.

"They called me," she says. "They called me to tell me that my father is dying. There's not one damned parking spot in this lot. Who the hell plows here? It's a travesty. I'm calling your company to report this. I had to park out on the street in front of that white house. Do you think they'll tow my car?"

"No," I answer, "it'll be OK there. It's not a problem. They won't tow it. If you'd like to leave me your keys, though, I can move it for you and find a space in the parking lot."

"No, that's alright, but if you can put a note on it for me, I would appreciate it," she says as she turns and runs into the building.

"Who is that?" asks the Administrator.

"Mr. Johnson's daughter," I reply, my heart kicking up a beat, thinking of her pain.

It has snowed every weekend since December 19th. We haven't had snow like this ever. We broke the record on Tuesday, fifty-nine inches in one winter. It has snowed so much that the plows can't keep up with scraping. The city and county have run out of salt and chemicals. Snow shovels can't be found in stores, and the roads get narrower as the latest white stuff gets pushed up against the last roadside mound. Our community comes together when crisis hits, but it seems we can only take so much.

Robert is our maintenance assistant. He is a farmer first, a maintenance man second. On snowy mornings, the cows get their breakfast before Robert comes to work to help feed old people.

He is forty years old, has never married, and has worked at the nursing home since he was sixteen. The care facility is as much a part of him as the farm, but in his life, priorities have four legs and hooves.

"They can't talk," he says, "someone has to make sure they are alright. Daddy's gone and so is Uncle Harold. That someone is me now. I'll be in after I feed."

Robert scrapes the nursing home driveway. He uses a 1957 John Deere Tricycle Tractor with a yellow blade attached to the three point hitch. It was his Granddaddy's tractor and he calls it "Putt-Putt." It used to live on the farm, but has traded in hay fields for city life. When he plows, staff and residents come outside just to watch Robert on the tractor. Old men remember.

When snow falls, Robert gets up early, feeds the cows and comes to town to plow the parking lot. It doesn't matter if it's a weekday or weekend, if it's Robert's day off, or if it's the fourteenth day in a row that he's worked. He gets in his truck and comes to the nursing home to plow the parking lot. He has been to work almost every day since December 19. He and Putt Putt have plowed snow and piled it out of the way the best way they can. With that, parking is at a premium.

I go in the nursing home and collect a piece of paper from the front desk. In bold letters, I write on it:

Owner needed to park car here in an emergency. If there is a problem, please come to the nursing home and inquire at front desk before towing. Thank you.

After placing the note on the car windshield, I go back inside, and walk downstairs to Mr. Johnson's room. His daughter is sitting next to the bed with her father's hand in hers. Her head was bowed. I knock quietly. She looks up, tears running.

"Can I get you something, a cup of coffee?" I offer.

"No, thank you," she says. "This is so hard."

"I know," I offer, but can't give her any other comfort. I feel helpless.

Turning away, I walk down the hall and see Robert coming toward me.

"Can you believe they're calling for snow on Monday?" he asks me, smiling, "like we haven't had enough. Where am I gonna put it?"

"I don't know, Robert," I say, "we're running out of room. The parking lot's full."

No Saint

by Bruce Reisner

(Mature: some coarse language)

A thick pea soup. I am not eating any of it, just now, nor is there a bowl of any kind in front of me. There seems to be a wishing well of thick green substance filling my fields of vision. I've been bruised, not physically, but assaulted. It has been raining all day, seemingly a green driving chilly broth. Cuffs and socks are still wet from a long hike in a harsh, didactic rain.

There was no indication at the bus stop a block from home that space and sound would befoul. No one in my part of town dressed for the occasion, or cared that it was happening. This isn't a popular holiday in a predominantly black lower middle class hood, and I feel better about this now than usual. The ride from there to downtown was the last thing about which I have no complaints.

The first omens were green trapezoids on thin young men, walking toward me on the sidewalk. Their jerseys showed through the brush of pedestrians not dressed for Saint Patrick's day. Too, people stood outside of restaurants and office buildings to smoke, wearing floppy hats, top hats, blinking electric antennae, loutish broaches and cheaply tailored kilts, all Kelly green. But that was in the late afternoon, between the smiling parade and the succeeding mass bacchanal. I had some socializing to do, movie and beer with a pal, and neither of us celebrate anything but days unmarked with patina so cruel as today. The trip to there was just enough of other people's festivity to cause flash backs of one brutal mass observance or the next. It was later, after dark, on the way home that I was made to remember how many brutes adore Saint Patrick, booze and mobs. I had to walk along Carson Street from the Hot Metal Bridge to Tenth Street in the thick of the raining human pea soup, and now my spleen must disgorge. But first the memories that staggered drunk and sick into flashbacks.

It was my maiden year in Pittsburgh, and I was innocently waiting tables in a dive restaurant on Carson. This street is always a fine backdrop for people to front in current fashion, and I like it, usually. Not just now, though. As usual, it had escaped me that the day was special, and this bad trip I suffered began with two yuppies walking in with a cardboard box. They were the glee captains for one of many neighborhood booster clubs, and the box was filled with Kelly green gear.

According to the chipper, well-heeled captains, he and she, a congress of interested parties wanted all the bar and restaurant staff along Carson, in a row like artificially dyed ducks—to wear a heavy array of holiday gear—all in my least favorite color. Property values stood to go up if the area looked like it was uniformly festive and culturally piquant. The staff in the dive that day were: the big oaf boss, a young unimpressive waitress, and my similarly second string self. There were trendy upscale restaurants, staffed with stunning and deft people, and common misfits could find work in the less popular holes. It was God's gift to free enterprise. Then, 1991, was among the last years for its greater glory.

The boss graciously accepted a pair of wide elastic suspenders and matching Skimmer hat. Green Styrofoam for the rakish schmuck. Plump and cooperative waitress failed elegance in donning a blinking Lucite headdress and matching battery concealed broach. She had taken upon herself to come to work in green skirt in the color to which I am averse. There was no dress code, and like many arch conservative fuck ups, I was happy in the clarity of black pants and a white shirt. I was trying to wait out the assault, passive resistance-like. I even tried hiding in the kitchen, but the boss called me out. The yuppies really wanted everyone on the floor in the party.

25

A name tag and bow tie. That was the least shit I could get away with on my physical being, the figure, the self, the carrier of some fishy yet valued escutcheon. An ethnic hold over with mustache and shifts to native language, the boss came there in deep red slacks that clashed like Gettysburg with the suspenders. His golf shirt lined up like the Brits against the hat, and he was clumsy on a good day. Electric waitress clashed with simple hard wood and some decent racks of glassware. The decor, in general, was good enough, and that small signifier was drowned in the sea of taped up paper party paraphernalia. That night became trauma because all night I had to serve delightfully tipsy bourgeoisie parakeets. This demographic brought garish gentrification to row houses and puzzle boxes of apartment subdivisions. Enemy to form and content. Enemy to purists. Enemies. They were well to do, trendy 'neo-urbanites', all delighting in the ethnic diversity made flesh by green stained schmucks like me. That was the beginning, the sliver that ends in gangrene.

The pouring of wine is beautiful when people are not improperly dressed, and even just a perky tie and tag with clovers is enough to fuck it up. Prisoners of war are sometimes forced to work as servants. Done, like I lost a boxing match.

A few years later, I got the working class and rowdy bridge and tunnel crowd sharing with me their lust for life. Again, I forgot it was Saint Paddy's day, had a pounding hang over for no reason at all, and had to walk two miles to an Avis car rental store. Again I will try to plan trips on days other than green alcoholic hell. That day was a harrowing hike through smiling, screaming, hooting, vomiting lugs of both sexes. Suffice here that this pea soup was the Pittsburgh blue collar, at its worst, festooned for the day in green. Their collective work ethics came out in the fresh air with their triple-the-driving-limit breath. Jesus himself might agree that wife beaters and ex-cons are among the salt of the Earth. I'm an atheist and have a substitute word for 'salt.' Four letters, starts with 's.' Walking fast as possible, eyes averted from Man, nerves a Tesla coil of pulsing pain. Then there was the rental office incident.

I sat in the office, in one of three gray chairs, like the ones they used to have in unemployment offices. There were a few people ahead of me, waiting to get out of the sauntering urban blight. There was a view of the street out the front plate glass window, and just as I got up to the desk to get my car keys, something caught all eyes.

A peppy red hatchback had tied to its roof a lumpy, ill formed hollow Statue of Liberty about seven feet long, lying like a rape victim on its side, bound to the shitty little car and spilling outward over front and rear windshields. Ugly. Ugly. Ugly as a drunken brutal mob. The car was stopped in traffic, and clear as the pain, there were four smiling assholes filling the interior, all dressed in Kelly green. Like their toadied mock up of Liberty.

As the pleasant young woman behind the counter prepared some paper work, one of the others in the rental office commented, "I wonder if they made that statue themselves."

In my abject, driven surliness, I shot back, "They probably stole it."

What followed was less arduous than, say, an intake interview at a state hospital, but veiled and professional opprobrium came upon the clerk. Her voice shifted from that of cheerful ticket taker to one of concern for public safety, as perhaps, too, a bartender may have to shut off a drunk before he kills someone with his car.

"Sir, are you carrying a gun?" she asked, with the trace of a smile, but the gravitas of civic responsibility was there.

It is here that I must plead for understanding. I didn't ask to be born beady, pinched and hollow looking, and with a hangover, I don't look like someone you'd meet at a church picnic. A peek at my drivers license photo reminds friends of the no fly list. I was forced by need for balance to explain to her that I was having a terrible day, was unarmed, not violent, not unable to drive like a church deacon. I got the car, and a case of the heebie-jeebies. The force of a loud green holiday can reduce a man to this sort of contrition and alienation. The drive out of town was haunted with the hideous statue, the howling, hooting, barfing smiling crowd, the color that makes me ill. Now today. Today, like the migraine given me by people.

Today. Today Saint Patrick's day taught me of the opposing forces in the circle. Both paisleys were ruffian. There were phalanxes of police spaced form block to block, as many as could be spared from the usual domestic murder details and outdoor mugging investigations. Revelers filled the side walk and the endless bistro tables in front of shamrock spattered bistros. As the party crowd watched or ignored it, arrests were being made in the street at about four crime scenes per quarter mile. The officers were blue, professional and versed in sadism, as were the green, motley, hoi polloi. To contrast the neat array of arrests in progress, there were as many unchecked arguments and fights spaced apart at least one per block

Had it been possible to catch a bus at any of the stops along the main drag, I would be happier than now. Each time I attempted to wait for a bus, the stop would over fill with thugs. I was not wearing anything green, and it was being noticed with rancor, the way ants look at ants that don't belong in their hill. I look about as Irish as Aunt Jemima, so that wasn't helping my status either. Suffice I belong to a dark skinned ethnic group, and was not in tolerant company. People were looking at me like I was a deer in buck season. Suppose the ugliness of the crowd kept me walking fast, eyes averted from the Kelly green thugs and navy blue cops, all of whom seemed not to like me. At the Twelfth Street bus stop a leering four hundred pound man was deliriously pissing on the side of a red brick bistro, his loud spatter mixing with the cold rain. His gang was sprawled in the munchkin sized brick commons, puking, arguing, deciding if their argument should come to blows. At the next stop I came to a gang converged on me, smiling, soused and looking for a victim. Had to walk faster yet to get to the next unacceptable bus stop.

The full force of alienation and fear came with the realization that one can be beaten to a pulp anywhere, anytime, as opportunity presents, for reasons of benign incompatibility, by ordinary people loaded with alcohol and rage. Police can dole out some lumps and taserings for breaking the law. Or for looking like someone who might. This yin and yang of law and lawless took me higher on the dizzy maypole of understanding. The world is at a balance, and light loads like me can get popped like a zit between the two sides that represent it.

This can't happen again for another year, but the message in the bottle floats in the same green water, the same pea soup, as well, on days other than Saint Patrick's. Perhaps I deserve all this. I'm not the most personable motherfucker on Christmas, either.

Crossing the Border
by Sheila Cano

I

My uncle crossed the border before he was born. In the dark of night, Juan, Gabriela and their four children, plus Pete in utero, rode a freight train from Mexico to the U.S. They left because Gabriela's brother had been shot by the Federales for letting Pancho Villa stay the night. Gabriela gave birth to my uncle in 1911, the first member of the family born an American. Three years later, my father, born in Fresno, became the first Californian.

II

When I crossed the border into Tijuana, I saw the dirt streets, the tin-and-cardboard shacks in the riverbed, and I wept. I thought, "there but for the grace of emigration go I." I couldn't bear to haggle with the shopkeepers over prices - everything was so cheap already, and I was aware of my comparative wealth. I had just stepped out of my cocoon, my sheltered life as a college student.

III

I drove across the border into Canada in my '62 Pontiac Tempest, a four-cylinder job with a two-barrel carburetor. I had used it to commute to university in San Diego: twelve miles in nine minutes. Now it was crammed with worldly goods, beginning a new life as we were.

"How long are you planning to visit?" smiled the Customs and Immigration officer.

"Oh, about two weeks," I smiled back.

"OK. Enjoy your stay."

The baseball in my throat shrank to the size of a marble by the time we got to Vancouver.

IV

As I stepped off the metal stairway onto the tarmac, I could barely feel my feet touching the ground. That was thanks to the Bloody Mary I'd had instead of dinner, on my first jet flight. Moping about leaving California didn't do me any good either; tears led to fierce pain in my ears as we descended. I could hardly hear the Customs and Immigration officer speaking, "Would you go into that room over there, please?"

Four of us gathered in the room. The others, two men and a woman, were East Indian. Like me, the woman had her long black hair in a single braid down her back. We filled out forms, answered questions, and I ended up with a visitor's visa. Despite the muggy August heat, a chill went through me. I felt as if I'd just been told by the sheriff, "You got six weeks to get out of town, kid." How to begin a new life with that cloud hanging over my head?

A month later, I went to the Immigration office downtown to try to renew the visa. My naive honesty, in response to the carefully crafted questions, unwittingly revealed the presence of my fiancé, who was hiding in Canada. I was refused an extension of the visa unless I brought him to the office for questioning. I could feel my scalp tingling as I left the building and returned to our seedy little attic apartment.

I contacted the Peace Center in town, and they advised me to get to the border without delay, turn in the visa, and try to re-enter Canada without acquiring another visa. I took the bus to Bellingham, handed over the expired document at the border, and phoned the number I'd been given. Two young women, students at the university, came to pick me up at the bus station. I stayed with them overnight, in their communal house not far from the campus. Another guest that night was a draft-evader from

34

Virginia, a soft-spoken guy who had been turned back at the border the day before when he tried to enter Canada by bus.

In the morning, the students packed us into their station wagon, along with a couple of other friends, and drove to the border. They put the draft-evader's suitcase in the spare tire compartment in the back, and I covered my overnight bag with coats. When we got to the crossing, the officer looked at us suspiciously, but seemed satisfied that we were just a bunch of students coming up to Vancouver for the day. If heartbeats could have been heard by the naked ear, the car would have been thumping like a bongo-drum concert.

It all happened so fast and suddenly we were free. We waited until we were well past the Customs building before letting out whoops and hurrahs. The Virginian and I knew that the girls were really angels of mercy who had shepherded us through the gates to freedom. I took him to the Peace Center before we parted company in Vancouver.

Now I was incognito once again, a non-entity in Canada, or you could say, just another illegal. I took a deep breath of relief, and came home with the good news. To celebrate, we walked over to the Dairy Queen on East Hastings, and each had a 20-cent ice cream cone, dipped in chocolate.

"I notice ya got California plates on yer car," croaked Mrs. Galvin. "Ya know, I lived in the States half my life, and I can tell ya, I know what the rules are. Ya can only stay for six months if yer a visitor, then ya gotta leave. I had a guy from Texas livin' here one time, an' I told him, I says, 'Ya can only live here for six months, and then I'm gonna call the Immigration Office.'"

V

Our neighbor, Neal, and I drove down to Seattle one day. There was a sale on at the university bookstore, and an art show we wanted to see at the museum downtown. When we got to the U.S. border, the officer inquired as to our citizenship. I said I was a U.S. citizen, and Neal showed him his British passport.

"Where do you work, Susan?" he asked.

"At Simon Fraser University," I answered.

"Would you pull your car over and park in one of those spots, please?"

He asked us to get out of the car, and to open the trunk. He searched there first, lifting the floor covering to check the spare wheel well. Then he got inside the car, looked in the glove box, under the seats, under the floor mats, and finally, he emerged.

36

"OK. You can go on now," he said.

"Would it be possible to ask what it was you were looking for?" I ventured.

"Oh, contraband."

"Contraband?" I puzzled.

"Oh, newspapers, printed matter, that kind of thing," he replied.

"Oh, I see."

We got back in the car and drove off. I recalled hearing that Black Panther Party newsletters and leftist literature, freely available in Canada, were considered subversive in the States. Later I found out that several staff members from Simon Fraser had been smuggling the papers into the U.S. Even though the literature was published south of the border, it was hard to distribute outside major cities. Some of the newsletters were sent to Canada and ultimately found their way back to the States in small batches: concealed weapons, as it were.

VI

Then there was the time my brakes failed. I was driving back from a day trip to Seattle with some friends. We went to see

Fellini's latest film, "Satyricon", rode the monorail, and had dinner at Ivar's Acres of Clams. A real Seattle day.

As we neared the Canadian border crossing, I slowed down and began to brake. But nothing happened! I pumped the brake pedal like you're supposed to and put the shift lever in neutral. No pressure. Now what? The building was about a block away, and there were several cars at each booth. I could just imagine the humiliation of rear-ending a bunch of cars at the border.

"Oh boy, no brakes," I said.

"Wha-a-t?"

"Oh, no!" shrieked my passengers.

"Pump the brakes!"

"What do you think I'm doing?"

I wasn't going very fast, maybe twenty miles an hour, and it was a slight uphill approach, which was in my favor. I figured since there was no one close beside me, I could crank the steering wheel and come to an inertia stop sideways, like you do on skis. Or, I could throw the shift lever into reverse and trash the transmission, but avoid hitting anyone. Then, I remembered the emergency brake. That's what it's for, right? An emergency. But what if the cable broke? All these thoughts whirled through my head as I pumped to no avail.

"Well, here goes nothing," I announced to my companions.

Slowly I pulled back on the brake lever, not wanting to do it too fast and jerk the cable. To my great relief and eternal gratitude, the mechanical principle worked, and the car slowed dramatically. I continued to depress the brake pedal, let up on the hand brake and used the pedal with new-found pressure. Though I nearly had to stand on it, the car did stop before the booth, before hitting the car ahead.

The officer, of course, was unaware of the little scenario that had just taken place. I don't recall the transaction, only that we came through quickly. Now: would the brakes work the rest of the way? I cautiously got up to highway speed, then tested them. They seemed to function almost normally—I wasn't having to stomp on them. We made it home OK, but it was a long thirty miles.

VII

At a dusty, dingy liquor store in Ensenada, I bought a bottle of tequila with a worm in it. This is hilarious, I thought, as I handed over my $4.00. I'll have the only bottle of tequila with a worm in all of Vancouver. It actually looked more like a caterpillar to me.

When we got to the U.S. border, the guard asked if we had purchased anything in Mexico. I cheerily volunteered that I had bought a bottle of tequila.

"Do you realize that you're not allowed to bring alcoholic beverages from Mexico into California?" he glared at me.

"No, I didn't realize that. We're from Canada," I replied.

"Well, I'm sorry, but you'll have to leave it here," he said.

"But we won't be opening it in California - it's a souvenir to take back to Canada," I argued.

"I'm sorry, Ma'am," he shook his head. "We have to confiscate any liquor purchased in Mexico."

Reluctantly, I handed him the bottle. It was then I noticed a stainless steel fixture beside the officer's booth. It looked like the kind of drinking fountain seen in department stores, a narrow rectangle about three and a half feet high. I watched morosely as he poured the contents into the sink. I saw that every booth, across ten lanes of traffic, had such a fixture. I imagined a funnel underneath, filling a bottle below.

When I got back to Vancouver, I discovered a different brand of tequila, with a worm, at the liquor store. The caterpillar was smaller and the bottle cost twice as much.

VIII

Dark hills loomed against the starry desert sky as we drove through northern Mexico. At Tecate the brewery twinkled, festooned with lights, issuing steam into the night air. The radio announcer hit a reverb button and hollered down a train tunnel about the virtues of used cars on sale. We stopped at a roadside restaurant for a cup of cafe con leche, drinking in the homespun atmosphere along with the warm breath of chicory. Blue and green painted tables and chairs nestled next to pinkish-orange walls, neon beer signs illuminating the place just enough for tired truckers' eyes.

Late in the evening we pulled into a motel outside Mexicali, the entrance in the stucco wall allowing only one car to pass through at a time. In the foyer of our room, a blue bulb glowed softly over a round coffee table and two big Naugahyde swivel chairs. The space that held an air conditioner in the summer had an electric coil heater which took a little of the chill off the room. A blue-and-white tiled shower was easily seven feet square.

At 6:30 a.m. we awoke to the wheezing trumpets and booming drums of an off-key military marching band. The army barracks were right next door to the motel. After checking out, we bought breakfast buns at a bakery in town, then wandered through the Mercado looking at souvenirs. The textiles, pottery animals and birds were irresistible, so we purchased as many as we thought we could bring back on the plane to Canada.

A huge lineup filled five lanes at the border crossing. We waited at least half an hour for our turn to be scrutinized. The U.S. border guard looked at my Canadian driver's license, at the California plates on the new Dodge sedan, peered at me closely.

"Where did you get this car?" was his first question.

"Oh, it belongs to my father-in-law. He loaned it to us for the weekend," I replied.

"Boy, you got a nice father-in-law," he grinned, his blue eyes relaxing. "Are you bringing back any gifts?"

"Yes, a whole trunk load—just about," I said. "Would you like me to open it up?"

"Sure. I'll take a peek," he said.

I got out and unlocked the trunk. He looked briefly at the pile of serapes and carefully wrapped ceramics.

"Wow, you weren't kidding! Okay, have a good trip," he laughed, and waved us on.

IX

After my mother moved to Bellingham from California, I used to take the bus down to visit her on weekends. At the U.S. border, we all got off for questioning, while a Customs inspector checked the interior of the coach. Not everyone was interrogated, but I always was. When they punched my driver's license number into the computer, a lot of information came up. They couldn't refuse to let me in, as I was a U.S. citizen. But apparently my life was of some interest to them, and I usually had to wait several minutes while my documents were scanned. At first it made me nervous, but I got used to the routine after awhile.

One time, I got on the bus in Vancouver and sat down beside a native guy. There were lots of empty spots, but all the window seats were taken. We were silent most of the way. However, as we approached the border crossing, the man clapped his hands to his head and mumbled to himself.

"Something the matter?" I asked.

"Aw, I just remembered. There's a bench warrant out for me in Whatcom County, for breaking and entering," he groaned. "I'd forgotten all about it - it was two years ago."

"Never mind," I said. "Just stand behind me in line and they won't pay any attention to you. They'll be too busy with me."

"Really? What did you do?"

"I was married to a draft dodger once," I replied. "But I've never done anything they could arrest me for."

As usual, we filed off the bus into the building. I was about tenth in line, and when it was my turn, the officer typed in my driver's license number. We stood there for five minutes while paper spewed forth from the printer, piling up on the floor. He began waving people around me without questioning them, and the native guy went over to sit on the bench with the others. Finally the officer said I could go, and we all got back on the bus.

"Gee, thanks a lot," the man said as we sat down again.

"No problem," I said. "It happens every time."

X

I handed my driver's license to the U.S. Customs and Immigration officer at the airport in Vancouver. My flight to San Francisco was due to leave in half an hour.

"This isn't good enough," he frowned. "Don't you have anything with proof of your citizenship?"

"No," I replied. "My Canadian citizenship card had my former married name on it, and I changed back to my maiden name, and I haven't replaced it yet."

"So you're a Canadian citizen?" he inquired.

"I was born in the States, and I later took out Canadian citizenship," I nodded. "The U.S. consulate said I might have dual citizenship, I don't know."

"Where were you born?"

"San Francisco, California."

"Well, we really aren't supposed to let you in without proper I.D."

"I didn't think it was necessary when traveling between Canada and the U.S.," I persisted. "I've never been asked for it before, and I've been going down there for more than twenty years."

"That's only because the officer chose not to ask for it," he bridled, "not because it wasn't necessary."

I pictured myself missing the flight—a non-refundable ticket, too. The air conditioning cooled my clammy forehead.

"Well, look," I pleaded, exasperated. "Just punch up my driver's license number and you'll find out everything about me."

His slim face pursed and pinched, and his dark eyebrows knotted as he worked the keyboard. He studied the monitor for about fifteen seconds.

"Okay. You can enter this time," he said stiffly, "but it's the last time you're allowed in without proof of citizenship."

"All right, thank you," I smiled. "I'll be sure to have the proper identification next time."

I hefted my bags off the inspection conveyor belt and trudged over to the baggage-loading belt. I reflected that I actually thought of myself as a citizen of North America, with roots in Mexico, California, and Canada. Part of a northward pattern of migration on the continent. What was next? Siberia? I don't think so, but I would like to go to the Arctic Circle one day. Take a plane to Tuktoyaktuk, and see the midnight sun.

Build a Green House
by M Dawn Thacker

Our community needs a Green House. Not one for gardening, but one for growing the lives and minds of frail, dependent, elders. One that promotes cultivation of people in a warm environment. Currently, too many of our seniors with physical and cognitive challenges are planted in cold warehouses.

Two of my grandparents died in nursing homes. They had no choice. My grandfather had a massive stroke, lost the use of one whole side of his body, his speech, and his ability to control bladder and bowel. Days spent in a wheelchair, dribbling food and drink from the corner of his mouth, trying to speak with his eyes alone, made my grandfather the saddest person in my life. I visited and tried to bring a little light back into his existence, but failed in my attempts. I always left him, crying. A lifetime of fly fishing for trout, growing Beefsteak tomatoes in his garden and building homes from the ground up, only played as old movies in his head. No one in the nursing home talked to him about his life; no one knew; no one cared to know.

My Grandmother lost her mind to dementia. She didn't recognize me. Looking through me, she mumbled words that made no sense to either of us. She dressed in backward layers and searched for home. In her day, she raised five children, cooked meals that fed not only her own family, but others in the neighborhood who were hungry. She pieced quilts to keep those she loved warm, and braided my long hair while telling me stories of her childhood. To the staff in the nursing home, she was a wrinkled body that had to be fed, bathed, and chased down the hallway because she wandered, looking for purpose.

When my great-grandparents were elderly and unable to live alone, they spent six week intervals with each of their nine children. When the elders visited, they helped as much as they could with cooking, cleaning, watching the children, doing yard work and small repair jobs around the house. When they were no longer able to be of assistance in a physical way, they used their knowledge to share recipes and gardening hints. They rested in rocking chairs, and at the end, took to the bed until it was time to 'go home.' Family gathered at the bedside, caring for basic needs and listening to last stories. When God and others before them called, this generation was sent to the next life surrounded by love. Nursing homes didn't exist.

48

In the 1960's family units began to change. Women worked outside the home and children no longer lived in close proximity to their parents. Something had to be done with Mom and Dad when age took their bodies or minds. As elders became unsafe in their own homes—leaving pots on the stove, wandering winter streets at night with no shoes, forgetting to eat—families, children, and communities, needed a 'safe' place. There was no model.

The early architects of nursing homes looked to the hospital as their model. Semi-private rooms, long halls, starched staff, polished tile, stainless steel, and shiny linoleum suddenly became 'home.' Kitchens were placed far away from living quarters. No one's mouth watered from the smell of baking biscuits. Laundry swished and swirled in industrial machines and came delivered in folded stacks, with a scent of Clorox. Baths, meals, therapy, activities and laxatives came on a set schedule. For the sake of safety, doors locked, walking discontinued, bodies with weak legs were tied down and when voices rebelled, chemicals in the form of antipsychotic pills hushed them. In caring for elders, quality of life was sacrificed. Staff 'cared' the life right out of the wisest ones.

During a visit to the 'home,' visitors met with scenes of drooped heads, drooling mouths, calls for "help" and "bring me a

49

pair of scissors to cut this strap." Bingo was the only activity that promised a surprise ending in a long and tedious day. Elders didn't have a say in their care. Their feelings and knowledge were ignored. They suffered alone in a building filled with people rushing about, or vegetating.

Laws in 1987 tried to regulate care, bringing rights to nursing home residents. It's a sad commentary on a society that has to pass laws to protect its eldest citizens. Each of us has these civil liberties—we are born with them, but because of rampant abuse and neglect, Congress passed a 'Nursing Home Bill of Rights.' Included in this mandate were the following rights:

-to be treated with respect and dignity;

-to receive care, treatment, medicines, and services in compliance with laws;

-to be free from mental and physical abuse, restraints;

-to open and read one's own mail, have access to a telephone, and writing materials;

-to manage financial affairs;

-to enjoy privacy in one's own room, with a spouse and for the couple to share a room;

-not to be expected to work for room and board;

-to have personal belongings.

We, as youthful humans, take for granted and expect these rights. We become outraged if these freedoms are yanked from us. In 1987, fundamental human rights had to be spelled out and enforced in nursing homes. Legislators developed a three inch thick ream of rules to regulate care facility practice. Nursing homes became the second most regulated industry in the United States behind nuclear power plants. Twenty two years later, there is change, but not nearly enough.

The medical model still exists. Nursing home residents continue to suffer from loneliness, helplessness and boredom. Institutions are large and every room, every hallway, looks the same. Breakfast sits on the plate in a yellow mound. Lunch and dinner are ground into unrecognizable meats and vegetables. Sliced bread is the only piece of normalcy on the plate. There are few spontaneous activities, while choices are limited.

Elders are no longer tied down or given pills to shut them up, but body alarms have taken the place of restraints. If someone chooses to rise from a wheelchair and their legs refuse to hold them up, a screeching alarm alerts staff. In most cases, the noise startles the elder into moving too quickly, and they sprawl on the floor anyway. As soon as most residents arrive, they are presented with wheelchairs. The halls in the building are long and the walk to the dining room for meals is quite a hike for arthritic bones. Loss of mobility comes quickly. Loss of self comes even faster. A person's diagnosis becomes his name, his disability, a nickname, his frustration, and a staff member's annoyance.

"There's a new admission in 208, he's a fractured hip, a feeder, and a screamer at night."

Not all facilities are warehouses for broken, old people. A reform movement called 'Culture Change' is making some progress. It's slow in coming, but all needed change seems to crawl when it should sprint. The main principle of culture change is person centered care. Individuals in these homes are encouraged to thrive in a community environment, not decline. 'Home' becomes the operative word, not the residence that each person remembers, but closer than the institutions that exist today.

A social model replaces the medical one. Each resident's room reflects her personality. Family photographs and artwork recognizable to the individual decorate the walls. Familiar furniture, a favorite chair, a vanity with a dresser set, and a four poster bed with a soft mattress make life more livable. Memory books, with cards and notes from children and grandchildren, stories from the past, and love letters from a spouse provide comfort. Residents choose when they wake, when they want to rest, what foods they wish to eat, and when they bathe. Staff members have consistent assignments—they learn the history, interests, likes and dislikes of the elders in their care. More importantly, the elders recognize their caregivers and relationships develop. Nursing assistants begin to understand that care is not the physical act of bathing and dressing, cleaning and making beds. Care is about the individual, and helping to make her life worth living.

"Clara helps me get dressed for the day, and then we can sit and talk a few minutes about the red bird couple visiting my bird feeder this morning," says Joan, a recipient of culture change care.

Unfortunately, the rules that came in the 1980's, designed to protect and care for elders, have discouraged a rapid jump into culture change. Administrators and Healthcare companies are fearful of the new direction. Regulations are strictly enforced and severe monetary penalties are imposed for noncompliance. 'Infection control', limits family style dining, homemade foods brought in by the community, and the adoption of pets. Medical care and treatment still supersedes a resident's right to eat and drink what he enjoys, or have a peaceful night's sleep without being awakened for turning, positioning, and care needs.

"I'm 96 years old. Sure I have diabetes, but I'd rather die from the sugar in a Hershey Bar than die from wanting one," says Earl, a three year resident in a care facility.

Staff are so concerned with documenting care, that they don't have the time to deliver it in a way that makes the resident feel like an individual.

"If services are not documented, they did not occur." This statement comes directly from a State inspector.

"Get it done, write it down, that's what I have to do in eight hours with a caseload of ten residents," says an overworked C N A. This rushed approach leaves the elder feeling like a piece of furniture to be dusted or a wilted plant needing water.

A forerunner of the Culture Change movement is The Eden Alternative. It's a small not-for-profit organization which is turning eldercare on its gray head. This organization embraces the belief that aging is a stage of development and a person can continue to grow well into the age of elder-hood. The Eden Alternative has developed new models for housing those in our society who are frail and dependent on others for care. These communities are called 'Green Houses'. They promote growth in their inhabitants. When an alternative Green House is built, instead of an institutional design with long foreboding hallways, smaller, residential housing units are organized. Each unit houses no more than ten private bedrooms with private baths. The rooms have doors that open to a short hall or a great room. Each house has its own kitchen, dining room, laundry, front porch, mailbox, backyard with grass, bird feeders, a cat or a dog, and a garden. There are upwards of fifteen units in a Green House community. Each house has ten elders, and a family of care staff. Residents can assist as they are able with meal preparation, cleaning, laundry, gardening, pet care—all activities they would normally participate in at home. Recreational pastimes, calendared events, interests and hobbies are pursued with passion or not, depending upon the likes of each individual. Elders feel needed, valued and activities are meaningful. Each house is run separately from the others. Each small community within the larger is autonomous.

Where are the nurses? Where are the administrators, social workers, business office personnel, maintenance workers, housekeepers, and dietitians? This innovative living concept does away with some positions. Those that are necessary are housed in a separate unit within the confines of the community. Care staff in the Green Houses are cross trained to provide personal care. Staff cook, clean, assist with activities, budget household expenses, and shop for needs. There is one 'Administrative Building', which houses offices and the nursing staff. Nurses travel from house to house like home health workers. They come at a specific time, provide medications and treatments, then leave. The housekeeper comes once or twice a week for deep cleaning, and the bed and bath linens are taken to a separate building for washing. They are delivered back to the house when clean, reminding elders of the old time laundry services. Personal laundry is washed, dried, folded, and ironed in each house with the assistance of the residents. The elders rule their homes. They plan meals, celebrations, spur of the moment ice cream making, trips to the store, or poker nights.

Green Houses in existence have waiting lists. The concept is innovative and studies show that elders thrive in these communities. Costs are lower, staffing needs are less, and quality time between elders and caregivers increases. With the Baby Boomer population reaching retirement age, society needs a new and better way to care for those who will be unable to care for themselves in the near future.

In a prime example, the City of Charlottesville prides itself on being a mecca for retirees. Cultural, educational, medical and community based services for seniors abound in this city. Yet, when a certificate of need is granted for an eldercare facility, an old medical model nursing home is built. Isn't it time that we, as an innovative community, take the reins in the Culture Change movement. Shouldn't we set the example of improved quality of life for our frail elders? Shouldn't we make the difference before we are placed in a medical model facility and wish we had done something about care when we had the ability?

Afton Mountain
by M Dawn Thacker

Afton Mountain is deceptive. When the sun shines, there's a clear view of Rockfish Valley on the eastern side. Cars become matchbox miniatures and vineyard rows look like fresh rake marks in dirt. Sometimes, visibility is so sharp that individual leaves on the trees wave to the passerby. On the western slope, the Shenandoah Valley spreads out rolling, slopes touching clouds, and dipping into ravines—a haphazard blanket over a bed of sleeping dogs.

When it's a gray day, and water droplets weigh down the pockets of the clouds, Afton Mountain is ominous. Fog rests in tree tops and filters down before sprawling on the highway, like a ghost with arms outstretched, quietly gathering up guardrails, warning signs, tail lights, cars, and whole tractor trailers in its mist. People become confused. Airplane pilots lose their visual bearings and travelers on Afton lose direction, front-to-back, side-to-side. It seems they drift alone and a silence takes over. The fog can kill.

In April 1992, sixty cars skidded then piled up on the mountain, claiming two lives. In April 1998, sixty-five drivers succumbed to the same fate; forty people were hospitalized. Three weeks later, eighteen cars collided in a chain reaction. When Afton Mountain hides under cloud, a dangerous game of hide and seek ensues. It's best not to be tagged. Stay at home when rain threatens.

Gina's Boudoir

by Gaboo

(Mature subject matter)

"Time reveals truth…"

Gina makes the proclamation and drops her bathrobe, stepping out of a velor lotus. A lamp frames her in light while she balances, one knee forward, wrists and elbows bent like you've just won a dishwasher. She's practiced the pose, and practiced seeing someone lying in front of her, watching. Two glossy, black dogs gaze past, oblivious. They're ceramic.

Gina's room is caked in trinkets. Fabrics drape around the bed and over the windows. Her delicates are piled on a chaise. The room's a shrine to bric-a-brac, and too much to absorb. Every surface is covered in ribbons and knick knacks. There's themed areas, like her teen years. She has a walnut dresser topped with wide-eyed figurines posing clumsy, courtship rituals. Center stage, a girl wearing a bonnet sits on a log. Her suitor thrusts out a bouquet, eyes closed, leaning in for a kiss. "Deal's a deal, Gina."

But she wouldn't see it that way. She doesn't understand crass. She sees an old boyfriend, or his return. Dollar store junk is her time machine and the room is a dream mill.

"Truth unveiled by time," I correct her, "Berlini or Bernini, bikini something…"

"Same thing."

"No it isn't. Time doesn't dig up truth—truth was already there."

"Either way," she cups her breasts with her hands, "truth is all I've got."

"So, I'm already here."

Lying on Gina's bed is like sprawling on a fairy game table. It's too high and she has too many pillows. My first instinct is to back paddle the fluff into a corner, but every angle is laced in ornaments. It's all junk, but treasures to Gina. She's shopped and collected a reality in knock off girlie. On the face of earth, a ten by ten room of Gina's delusions isn't so bad. The iron core can handle half a ton of denial.

That's why I bring her mementos, airport afterthoughts. I'm responsible for the shelf of delusion next to her wardrobe—colored chopsticks, a pen set, and a toy panda from China. She doesn't know how to use chopsticks and I doubt she'll ever write to China, but Gina remembers when I came back from Beijing and held her close in bed. She listened to my stories. I recounted the trip, the food—how I got around. I wished out loud that she had gone with me—or would—sometime. She doesn't need to go to China. She doesn't want to. Gina remembers she was asked. The invitation sits frozen on a shelf. If we argue, or she thinks I'm not listening, I'll look to the souvenirs. She follows and calms down. I never mention the other collections or ask about them. That would drag up bones. Her past is perfect where it sits, everything in place. I don't want to spoil the memory and I don't have the heart to tell her the earth will end.

"Well?" She's waiting for a response, still posing. Butter girl.

"You look fine."

"That's not very convincing," she says.

"You look good."

Gina picks up her robe, and walks to the treat pile. She glances over her shoulder with a rear-end wiggle, "Heels?"

"No, no nothing," I drift back. I'm not considering her feelings enough. She wants stay above simple, earthly distractions—somewhere enchanting. "Really, I just want a second to breathe. You're perfect. Let me look at you... get's me going."

Gina's not shy, but I think she's uncomfortable without gimmicks. She's stuck on glitter. Standing naked makes her clinical and she starts acting like a peeler. I want her to feel comfortable. I want her to feel like she can trust me.

I pat the bed, "Come and curl up, like we're in an igloo."

Gina's forty and looks it, even though she's blessed with younger skin. She feels natural, not cosmetic. I caught her still happy to tumble. She may have been lighter when she was younger, but her photos show full features. And I love her hair. She'll tie it up and prop a set of glasses on her nose. Then I'm whipped.

She slides beside me, rubbing her hands over my chest down to my waist, "Brrr... you're cold, baby, come here."

"You left me all alone."

"Yeah, but your circulation is definitely slow."

"You're just a heat thing. Warm me up."

Gina entwines without hesitation. When we started up together, I thought she was locking me in a wrestling hold, but I realized she uses all her might to get closer. As soon as she makes contact, her legs wrap around mine. Her arms loop around my neck and she settles in pillow position, facing me, nose to nose. Her breasts and belly press and she holds her breath, eyes shut tight, squeezing her arms and legs. She truly wants us to join, or she believes we can. How can she give that easy?

As quickly, she loosens, weaves her fingers into my hair and hikes up on my leg, straddling my thigh. Her eyes flash open, "OK, let's talk."

I relish her contentment. I don't want to bring up drugs because it leads us into accusations. I just want to know she's here. The lamp isn't bright enough to let me see where the mood ends and ceiling begins.

"I was thinking about plans—years ago—not make believe."

"Did you stop?" Gina's looking in my eyes. She's searching honestly, but not for an answer. She wants to see if she's getting through, if I'm malleable.

"Stop what?"

"Making plans, baby," concern's on her lips and her brow wrinkles. She's not wearing make-up and I like it. We lie like we're committed to a mortgage, trying to save for the kid's teeth, and we have a dog. We're trying to make it on one income, and she almost does it, takes me to a three bedroom rancher with a walk and a lawn mower, her lips cooing inches on the other side, the better side. She's the Gina who says, "it's OK, baby, we'll do fine." Gina's not wearing any make-up and that's for me. I get to rest on her eyes and I don't want anything between us. No barriers. I want her to admit this is real.

But all her words are too sensual, the ones you whisper in a new relationship. She wants us at the beginning of something. She wants us younger, ready to run away and flood the years. She lulls me into sexy, curling, on a pillow that's too large, wrapped in a body that's too soft—lying in a fucking dollhouse.

I inhale her breath and speak it back, "Do you think we're where we're supposed to be?"

That sounds like I'm lecturing, "I mean, do you ever wonder if you missed out on something?"

"Are you asking if I'm happy?" Gina's not puzzled. She's up for games, if they're light.

"Or just satisfied…" I'm hesitating, leading.

65

"Babe, would you feel better if you were somewhere else?"

It wouldn't matter. Maybe if I was someone else, but there's no way.

"I think I would always be the same—inside—just different circumstances."

"Well, I know I wouldn't want to be anywhere else," Gina's still posing. Her pronouncement makes everything alright. She's not catching on and slipping. God, I crave reality. I'm so tired of pretending, restricted. If we were married, everything would be better. There wouldn't be bliss, but there could be something near normal. Except she wouldn't be happy. And I doubt I ever will. I realize I'm scowling.

Gina moves her fingers over my chest, finding the seam where our bodies fold. Her hand slips between us, catching scent and then traces back to my face, over my lips. She's gentle. She wants me immersed.

"Anything?" she whispers.

"Don't ask that right now, please... This is all I need."

That was too abrupt. Start again, "This is everything, baby... all I need."

"I don't want to get you upset... I just thought we were there. I felt us. Didn't you?"

"Yeah, we are, baby. Don't change anything."

She closes her eyes again and kneads into my shoulder. Rest, Gina. Just let me know you can rest with me. Resting is real.

I must have fallen asleep.

Gina's talking, sitting on the bed in a skirt and sweater. She looks thick, a phone in her hand, laughing. The curtains are open and gray afternoon is a blunt weapon. I listen to her voice, but not the words. I'm in vibration, fluttering between fear and contentment. Gina makes it softer. Keep talking, baby. She's interfacing with the world. She's getting the update from another mom—our kid is playing with a friend. We're stealing a little time, hidden in the spare bedroom, her trinket room. We set it up just for us. Now she's on task, being mom so I can sleep. Could I love her? I don't want to stray there—shut the thought away.

"Babe," she crosses her hands over the phone and holds it to those heavy breasts, like she's holding a bible, "I've gotta run out, just a bit. You be OK?"

"Yeah, I'm gonna go anyway."

"I put your catheter by the bag. There's a new one."

"Thanks. Thanks, Gina."

I'm awake. Thanks for crashing the dream, Gina. Don't dote. I want to throw the piss bag against the wall. It screws everything up when you act like you know me, Gina. But I don't say it. I want to smash and kick through the window. I want to hit the air and spin out from the eleventh floor—plunging my feet into concrete and exploding. All dead little pieces. Leave my piss bag, Gina. Leave it alone. Why do you screw everything up pretending? Stupid games. Can't you leave alone?

"Baby, you're shaking…"

I can feel the tears come.

"I'm just cramping…" My legs are trembling and the bed's starting to vibrate. Gina's familiar.

"I'll get your chair."

"Leave it, Gina, please…"

I know I'm sobbing, but I'm too mad to think, I want to be screaming mad dead. Can't she see?

No. Instead she's just there, with her arms around me, pulling me up in bed, grasping my head and turning my face, holding me under her chin. My neck's forced back; the position is uncomfortable. She squeezes because she's perfecting love. She read the manual. I'm here, in Gina's garden, and that solves everything. I hate it that she holds me.

"Would you ever marry me, Gina?"

"Now what would my daddy say, bringing home a young thing like you?"

"Your dad's dead."

She doesn't pause, "You know I love you."

"Yeah."

"And you love me... right?"

"Yeah."

"Don't be sad, OK?"

"I won't."

"I don't want to leave you here like this," she pulls back, making sure I understand the lesson, gripping my shoulders. No one else stays in the room when Gina's out. Not even to slit their wrists. I know I'm privileged, but for the wrong reasons.

"No, go, go. I'm OK. Everything's OK."

"You'll call me later? When you're home?"

"Sure."

She pushes off the bed, and stands looking at me, momentarily unsure, then smiles and picks up her purse, opens the door, and with a wave, she's gone.

I don't wait much longer and lift my legs over the side of the bed. She's laid out my clothes. Bless her.

I can't wash at Gina's, the chair won't fit, but I unwrap the catheter and get it inserted. I drain without realizing.

Keys. Jacket. Wallet.

She'll need some money. Food. Bills. I count out two hundred and wheel to the dresser. The ornament sits center stage, the young girl wearing frills, seated on a log. Her suitor offers a bouquet, eyes closed, leaning in for a kiss. I always leave it here—the money—slid between the lovers. Gina won't catch on. She doesn't understand crass.

Open the door and spin around, one last check before I roll out.

Everything's the way she likes it, dreamy. Dreamy and nothing's true, like when you think you love someone and time just stops. It's liberating leaving.

The Space Between
by Adrienne S Moody

I'm told by a reliable source, my brother, that our family home has a sign on a window that reads: ***Abandoned.***

"Is it going to be bulldozed down?" I asked, upset at the thought.

"It doesn't say. It just says, 'Abandoned' and there are chairs, beds and such—strewn about—and a huge container on the front lawn."

My parents built this house when I was four years old. It's a bungalow featuring three small bedrooms upstairs and a basement, which in time, was finished with actual walls covering the wood skeleton. My eldest brother, Jon, had his own room, while Mark and Elliot shared a double bed on one side of the basement. There was only a concrete floor. (I just realized how tough it must have been for the two of them.) There was no wall separating their bed from the rest of the basement and I'm quite sure they shared sleeping arrangements until the eldest moved out. Then Mark took Jon's room and Elliot, after he acquired a girlfriend, moved into the furnace room for privacy—especially when he rigged up an electrical current to the doorknob when they wanted to be intimate.

I was given my own room as I was the eldest of three girls. I felt quite privileged and I am sure that fact alone fueled the war between me and Elaine. Margaret was the baby and trotted on smiling and gurgling, unaware of the chaos around her. Six children in a nine hundred square foot bungalow didn't leave a lot of room to move.

My room was purple. Purple rug, purple fabric curtains and light purple paint. Purple was psychedelic and it was the '60s. When the sun poured into my room, it entered a world apart from the rest of the house. Ice formed all around my window in the winter, and during the most frigid months I would stand on top the register and wait for the rush of heat to balloon up my nightgown, blissfully warm.

My sister told me, after we all moved out and my parents uprooted to a senior's complex, that during one of her visits home she saw a *For Sale* sign in front of our box of memories. She decided to do a walk through.

"What was it like? What stands out to you the most?" I asked, intrigued by her interest in the past, matching my own.

She paused.

"The sound of the door shutting."

"Explain. What do you mean?"

"Well, the rugs were different, the paint—they knocked a wall out and have two bedrooms upstairs now. The tile in the kitchen is different and the cupboards, too—but the sound of the front door shutting is the same."

I closed my eyes, envisioning. I could hear that sound, too.

And now this most recent news haunts me. I imagine how empty the home is, abandoned, without people or belongings. I wonder if there is anything, any evidence—a shred of wallpaper, a faded scribble—that my family once lived there. I wonder about the space between those walls. How quiet it must be.

Read This Please

Volume 1 Edition 2 - People Watching

April 01, 2010

Writers flock to the popular milieus to observe, characterize, and portray. Enter the people watchers. Have you ever considered that the last time you went to market you became the character in a story?

Bus Rider Portraits
by Sheila Cano

Every few months, I take my car in for service and ride the buses that day. Bus-passenger watching becomes my entertainment. Some characters stand out for me due to their manner of dress, facial expressions or posture. To wit:

This one I have seen before. He is middle-aged, bespectacled, bald, sports a black bandanna tied like a headband, and a shiny, well-worn black leather Outback hat that is a little too small for him, perched high on his head. Two rolls of fat hold the bandanna in place, one above and one below. A double row of metal badges and pins encircle the hat: a Canada flag, assorted souvenir pins, car logos, lodge pins, anything metal with colourful paint. His shirt, vest with bulging pockets, and pants are all greasy, dirty denim. A large round badge with a bright blue design adorns the vest. He wears another short black leather vest with laces up the sides, and on his sock-less feet are beat-up silver and black running shoes. He grips the metal pole beside his side-facing seat with one hand, his other hand clutching a large plastic shopping bag full of groceries wedged between his knees. I cannot see, but intuit that he must have a scuffed metal cowboy

76

belt buckle. Without moving his head, his eyes dart left and right to peer at the people around him. I imagine he is checking to see if anyone notices his flamboyant get-up. He is desperate for attention, but he does not speak to anyone. His clothing speaks for him. I think he lives in a group home, has a disability, but is functionally independent and rides the buses several times a day. As a kid, he dreamed of being a cowboy. He would be polite and friendly if I spoke to him.

She just got off the bus, carrying bags in each hand. Her large florid freckled face is surrounded by a halo of graying red hair. Her scowling facial features seem to be all on one flat plane, her nose pushed in like a Persian cat's. She wears a short-sleeved gray and white shirt and brown slacks. Anger and fear radiate from her like flames. I am glad I'm on the bus and not in her path. She probably never married, lives alone and has a part-time job as a cook at Burger King. She buys her clothes at the thrift store but lacks a sense of style. She is disappointed with her life, has few friends and most of her conversations are complaints and back-biting gossip.

In His Pocket

by Adrienne S Moody

Laura wasn't always a God fearing woman. The enlightenment happened in the 15th year of her marriage. Back then she was a scrapper and was known to throw dishes at the wall when her husband, Gerald, exasperated her beyond control. Their home, a battlefield and their three daughters would vanish upstairs under the covers at the first sign of trouble. It could be a plate slammed down on the table, or the oven door shut unnecessarily loud. Sometimes, their mother's voice changed ever so slightly and the eldest girl would nudge the middle child and raise her eyes to the ceiling. That was the cue to vacate. Now.

Laura was born near the Dead Sea, in a small resort town. Her parents owned a shop which kept them very busy and quite frankly this newborn child, Laura, caused them a great deal of stress what with all the crying and constant tending. They decided to let Antonio's sister, Edi, living on the other side of the country take her and raise her. It wasn't a difficult decision. Eliana did not take to motherhood. She felt great relief putting Laura into Edi's loving arms. They drove back towards home, their business, chatting animatedly about plans to expand.

Laura saw her parents once a year after that. When she reached the age of 13 her parents decided to move to Canada where opportunities seemed attractive and worth the uprooting of the family. Times had changed for their tourist town and they were unable to keep up with the times. Their old fashioned tea and coffee shop needed something they could not give. They refused to speak English and that only alienated them from the few customers who would poke their heads in.

They settled in Canada and opened a new business. Antonio decided a moving company was good honest work for the family. He had a strong back and the workers he hired spoke English well and he felt very little need to learn the new language. He pulled Laura out of the school she only just begun and instructed her on how to answer the phone. Laura felt relieved to not have to study any longer. Grade 7 work felt beyond her capabilities and she struggled so with reading and mathematics. But she could answer the phone and book her father's jobs.

Her father kicked her when she made mistakes. And she made many. He kicked her so severely in the buttocks that the muscle never healed and caused her great embarrassment in later years. A bathing suit could not hide the ripple and people always asked. Only to her closest friends did she reveal the truth. When they would gasp at the story of abuse, she appeased them, or tried to, by telling them that he meant no harm, he could not help his temper, that he really truly loved her.

When one of the employees continually performed poorly he would have to be fired. Antonio would instruct his young daughter what to say to the worker about to be canned.

"You tell him this, Laura. And you tell him in these exact words, "You are a stupid son of a bitch! You better not show your fucking lazy ass at our doorstep! You're fired!"

And Laura would. She wrote the words down, best she could, and with her heart beating so loud she could hear it, dialed the number her father gave her and repeated word for word the abuse.

So, back to her God fearing ways. She became a born-again Christian. She learned in her studies that a woman's place is to serve the man, a feeling she suspected was true. She only had to think of her childhood for proof of that. She soon saw her young adult years as rebellion from the word of God. She demanded so much from her poor husband, her mentor at church would shame her.

"So you think he should listen to you when you are troubled? You think he has nothing better to do, Laura? What troubles could you possibly have compared to him, your leader? Learn to silence that voice in your mind that tells you that you want more in your life. You are very lucky to have the man you do. Stop expecting so much. You must learn to be silent and to serve. When you do this you will receive God in your heart."

This is what Laura wanted more than anything. God. God would surely fill the emptiness inside of her. She went to bible study daily. She stopped complaining. She did her household chores and tended to their children without any negative words and soon the negative thoughts ceased. Prayer to God became her nourishment and she served her family the way the church taught its women and everyone around her, her husband, her children, smiled more often. The fighting stopped.

She became glued to her husband's side. Everywhere he went she asked to go.

"I sometimes wish I could make you tiny and put you in my pocket so I would never have to leave you at home. I could just reach in and pull you out to see you and put you back," he would tease her.

That is just how she felt, so tiny and vulnerable and scared to death to be left alone. Alone without him was surely death on earth. Then the worst thing imaginable happened. He became very sick and a year after diagnosis, died. The children were grown and out of the house with their own families. Laura was alone for the first time in her life. She could no longer be tiny and protected in her husband's pocket.

Every night she prayed herself to tears asking God for direction. She left all her deceased husband's pictures around the house and they were everywhere, in the bathroom, above the sink, in her bedroom on both sides of the bed. She talked to him constantly. She would call their cell phone to hear his greeting.

She longed to be tiny and protected in his pocket.

Watching Online
by Sarah Scott

Perhaps I'll never comprehend the drunken stupor of my friends. They call me mornings after, not recalling where they went, who they went with, or what they said. I'm amazed by alcohol's ability to make one forget. Take Cindy, for example, she's married, thirty-one, and last night she polled the room:

"What do you do when a child really wants to kill themselves?"

The replies were endless, and one elicited a shameful response. James wrote: "For insight, call me. I've been there."

Poor Cindy, in her mindless alcohol induced haze, replied: "I'm there tonight. I'm writing this while I'm drunk."

I called her today and told her about the post, how it could ruin her chances of finding gainful employment. The sad part isn't that she posted the question—it's a legitimate concern, we all wonder, especially those in the mental health field. The sadness comes from the fact that she had to ask "Did I really write that? Where?" She honestly couldn't remember.

I think she needs an intervention. She's such a sweet gal so full of life and spunk. I don't understand this part of her, this desire to drink beyond numb and into oblivion. I picture the horror on her face as she wonders what else she forgot. She thanks me, hangs up, and this evening she'll start again.

Observe the Male

by Gaboo

(Subtitles in Martian)

Azem

First off, some perimeters. Also, I will drift in conversation and perspective, addressing female readers and alternatively any male friends who may be following along. (Don't worry brother, I won't give away The Secret.)

Observe the male in social settings. His attention will naturally gravitate to the prettiest girl in the room. If a guy says he does not look, then he is lying, or blind, or a devout Taoist. Even gays will look and check the view. Pretty is pretty, and flowers get noticed. I explained this truism to my wife long before she was betrothed, and I also explained that my graphic nature made my reaction time instinctive.

Women I've known are also quick to lock radar on 'the belle'. It's some weird celebrity/popularity/competitive thing more than sisterhood or affection. But for every guy, beauty has different qualities. I've seen a fine woman pass a table of stags like a svelte frigate under sail, capturing adoration even if she was pushing

190. It's how she carries herself—how proud, how captivating. If you hear the confident click of sashaying heels on a sidewalk, watch the guys. Males can't *not* follow the sound to its source. Slick chicks come in various shapes and sizes—and they know just how to play it hot.

Er

For most guys, attention means 'a glance'. There's no need for acknowledgment. She wore the right cut of skirt, or her hair was willowy or she smiled off camera—he looks, categorizes the impression into a pretty folder, and moves on—there's a menagerie of images logged and forgotten in his brain cavorting in appealing legs, hips, dimples, eyebrows, and necklines.

In contrast, the image of his loved one is more like a fluid painting that fills his mind, and the glimmer of her smile and all the reasons behind it shine through. A man's wife becomes his eyes in a dream; he doesn't see her, he feels her presence in his thoughts--he looks at the world for her.

A guy in love is constantly wondering, "Would she like this? I wish she was here, I want to show this to her. What would she say?" —he builds a world for her everywhere he goes, until the wondering drifts behind a cute checkout girl. Then the wife's flagship persona manifests, rearing in blunt traffic warnings,

"Wife would not like this. Wife would not authorize this interaction."

The whole visual thing is a jigsaw of blurs. Blame fashion and media. The unprepared male is subject to sophisticated nuances of color, cut and skin. His small, reptilian brain stem was prepared for basic grunting, cooing, scenting, and identifying the squat of his mate in a meadow.

Kak

Note rules of order. For our society to avoid disintegration, women and men have a general understanding of behavior—nothing new. IF a buddy's wife looks hot—disregard. If the judge is female and looks hot—disregard. If anyone of an age that can get you arrested looks hot, or if your aunt looks hot—disregard. If you have not had this discussion with your wife or your intimate other—pretty much disregard everything. Avid glancing and she'll see your instinctive response as an affront, or worse, a compulsion. We have to train ourselves not to look. The majority of guys don't leer; they're just mesmerized, a touch dense, and breathe through their mouth when trying to gather information. Study apes in social opportunities. Likewise, if you have this frank discussion with your spouse, consider that her appreciation of beauty is hers alone. We all eye-spy the picturesque tree in the forest. There's nothing personal.

Bloot

As a courtesy, if a guy is married and glancing around too much, his buddy will casually ask if he's "gettin' any?" This strategy is done for the benefit of the wife, whom the buddy usually respects, as she successfully fills husband's time when buddy is busy or at work. Wives and their husband's friends master a delicate dance. They can see eye-to-eye on their mutual concern: Friend wards off potential threats; wife ensures friend gets clearance to see husband at most hours. So if buddy catches husband snooping the field, he identifies the hot issue quickly and reorientates the husband back to domestic safe zones.

"Whaccha lookin' at, finger lip smackin'?"

"Geez."

"Yep, havin' that. Nice...pick up the kids at school first."

"ah.. "

"Crash."

"Geez."

Thus, the topic of conversation between males quickly pirouettes back through wife, kids, marriage, work, automobiles, sports, music, and then into politics, government and the economy. This is the set, normal progression of discourse between two familiar males. The latter the topic on the discussion chart (ie. fiscal policy) the longer and more passionate the interchange. Women will flatter themselves, but guys—and especially ones over 40—really don't spend a lot of time discussing females. A fellow is either with his girl, or not.

"You and the wife go out last night."

"Yep."

Then the pause of familiarity.

"So what about the tax thing?"

"I know, those guys really tick me off. Here we go again...."

Sona

Sorry to jade anyone's sensitivities, but even religion gets more play between males. The problem is that most wives and girlfriends over-scrutinize the relationship. A buddy becomes a respite from the work of emotional bonding. If your man is nearby, then he is thinking about you. If he is not with you, then he is probably thinking about all-terrain tires, or kayak paddles, or helium balloons. A guy thinks on his girl when she is not where she is supposed to be—typically if she is not next to him when sleep comes. Even if a guy is cheating, after the roll in the sheets his brain goes directly to his wife. Most guys don't even know if they are being hit on by a woman unless the wife points it out.

Except, of course, single guys. They are rutting sharks—a constantly searching, after-shaving, cologning, mirror-gawking libido. Married guys quickly tire of the ever-prowling, manic, relationship woes of their unmarried friends. But single buddy's narcissism can be tolerated provided there's some quality time or help dropping in a motor. Romeo's babbling and dating escapades can be overlooked if the friendship has merit. Enough background information? Onward.

Mel

by M Dawn Thacker

When I first met Mel, I felt sorry for her. I thought of myself, and how I would miss my vision if it was taken from me by some force of fate. I imagined the sadness of losing the purple of my morning glories, the opaque green of the sea glass I search for at the shore, the rusty red of McIntosh apples in the fall orchard, and the four petaled white of dogwood blossoms in spring. What would I do minus the color in my world?

I love faces, watching them, admiring their differences, the way brows furrow, eyes crinkle at the corners, noses turn up on the end and how cheeks dimple with a smile. I study frowns when I'm sitting on a park bench and smirks at the food court in the mall. I know people think I'm forward, looking directly at them as I do, but I can't help myself. Faces fascinate me. If the power button to my vision was turned off, I would miss channel surfing profiles.

Sometimes, for no other reason than to ride, I get in my car. I turn left out of the driveway and find crooked gravel roads to places I've never met. I've discovered silver ribbons of train rail,

91

wooden bridges that clatter under my tires, fields of thatch and lavender thistles, old gray barns with red tin roofs, and dappled horses grazing by board fences. Without my eyes, these would be lost to me.

Mel had vision. It just wasn't in her eyes. I was surprised one day when she said, "Train, you are very tall."

"How do you know I'm tall, Mel?"

"Your voice is really far up there," she said from her seat in the wheelchair. "I'd say you were as tall as most men." She was right.

Mel loved to talk and called me to her room to discuss the news, complain about the villain in her favorite soap opera on TV, teach me a new song she learned, or a Bible verse she thought might help me with my latest life crisis. I was ashamed that I sometimes tried to sneak by her because my time was precious and I had work to do. She called to me when I turned the corner near her room in the nursing home. "How do you know it's me coming down the hall, Mel, when I haven't even said anything," I asked her one day.

"You wear soft soled shoes, Train. You don't make much noise, but your steps are far apart. Your legs must be long, no one else here has that kind of stride." Again, she was right. I couldn't fool her into thinking I was not there.

Mel's fingers were sensitive. She knew texture, like I knew color. "Your sweater is wool, Train. I know because the yarn is course and a little hairy. It scratches on my fingertips. What color is it?"

Why did Mel ask me about color? She was blind from birth, had never seen colors. In my mind, she wouldn't understand the concept. I didn't ask, just gave her the information she requested. "It's blue," I'd say. Finally, one day, my curiosity got the best of me. I asked her why she wanted to know about colors.

"I see colors in heat, and cool, smell, sound, taste and feel," she said.

"Oh," I said. "Tell me what you mean, Mel. It sounds interesting."

"OK, Train, here's how I see colors. Blue is running water. Yellow is the way the sun warms my shoulders when I sit on the porch. Orange is a sharp bite and twang, like when you peel a fresh piece of fruit and it spritzes you. Red is a crisp bite of apple. Green is the feel of soft moss growing on rocks. Tan is the grit of sand, and the way it feels slipping between my fingers. White is the softness of a cotton ball. Silver is a bell ringing, and black is the quietest quiet you can hear."

At that moment, Mel's world began to make more sense to me. I no longer felt sorry for her. Her vision was far superior to my own. I stopped seeing her as blind, and started seeing her as Mel. She died in 2003; I miss her wisdom and my lessons in seeing without eyes. I went to pay my last respects to her at the funeral home. She was wearing her favorite dress. It was the soft color of Mel's first puppy and the richness of her favorite dessert, gingerbread.

I took the story of Mel to a reading, the fifth writer in a group of six, and I was so nervous that I'm surprised I heard the other participants, but I did. I became engrossed in their stories and could have closed my eyes while they read to me all night, one five minute story at a time: a mother's lament about moving her children to England, where they felt lonely and out of place; the story of Hap, a boy who's mother died when he was ten, and his alcoholic father; Amy's story of fighting Chemo in her twenties; Brownie, Patty's Grandmother's story of growing up "Irish trash"; and Polly's story of generations gardening the same spot. My Mel story came after Patty's and before Polly's, T between two P's.

Two members of my class were also reading and my teacher was there holding us up with her enthusiasm. The MC, Polly, told me in an email that it was a small crowd by reading standards, a kind group of like-minded people. I didn't know because I had never been to a reading before. I was still scared. I knew three out of the twenty five people. No, I knew four, I had met Patty's husband, Jim.

I was so taken with Patty's voice, a true southern drawl that I hadn't even realized I was next. Time moved. I sat in the chair and listened to my grandmother talking to me in her sweet words. I was back in her bedroom, sitting on her lap in the rocking chair by the wood stove. The floor lamp shined over her shoulder onto the picture book and her sound carried the story to my ears. I was five again. "Brownie, you are so beautiful, make sure that the words that come out of your mouth are just as beautiful as you. Can you do that for your Mama, just once?" she asked.

"Train-Whistle," was the next thing I heard, and it wasn't my grandmother. It was the MC. I stutter stepped to the podium, announced my rookie-ism and started in on reading Mel. After the first paragraph, my voice got stronger and after another minute, it wasn't like I was reading at all. It was like my own words were just spilling out of me, with all the emotion and color

95

there was supposed to be. Mel came and helped me. I'm sure of it.

"It was the soft color of Mel's first puppy and the richness of her favorite dessert, gingerbread," I finished to the clap of an audience.

The MC invited us to have refreshments. She came up to me after the reading and patted my back, telling me that it was a beautiful story and I didn't sound nervous at all. She looked at me and smiled, saying, "Please try some of the gingerbread I made." Yep, Mel was there.

Lewd Balloons
by Adrienne S Moody

He reads meters for a living. That's his day job. The guys at work, and they are mostly guys, consider him affable enough and when they heard that he clowned on the side, it became something to joke about at first, but that snippet of info soon blended into the dullness of their workday. Ed's buddy, Jasper, suggested the idea to him after Ed's divorce left his bank account in the red and his emotions depressed.

"A clown? You figure?" he asked when the subject emerged at lunch in the coffee room.

"You learn a few tricks. You're kinda goofy anyway, Ed. You know Jerome? He works the south side?"

Ed nodded as he stirred psyllium into his orange juice.

"What are you doing, man? What is that crap?" Jasper made a disgusting sound and scrunched up his face.

"It's the purest form of fiber. It cleans me out." Ed gulped the thick mixture and clunked his glass down, "Yeah, I know him."

"He picked this up years ago. He advertises on Craigslist and he makes like $50.00 an hour doing kid's parties. He says it's a blast! He makes more moolah playing clown than this—let me tell you."

"Thanks for the tip. Maybe I will. How tough can it be to be a clown?"

Now, Ed was a do-it-yourself kind of guy, so he went online and researched clowning. He decided to specialize in 'Balloon Sculpting'. He found it fascinating how the hands moved so quickly. Out of nothing it seemed, someone could produce what he considered art. He bought a unicycle and in his empty living room—his ex took all his furniture—he practiced riding. He arrived at work with bruised arms and when asked about it he said it was all in the name of 'art.'

Within six months Ed had his costume, perfected his makeup, and mastered the unicycle. He could sculpt 25 different objects with balloons and learned the words to ten nursery rhymes. He already knew how to play the banjo, which rounded off his newly acquired talents nicely.

He missed family life. Sometimes at night after applying his makeup in front of a dressing table mirror, he'd gaze into his reflection, sadness would overwhelm him and he'd watch, fascinated, as tears roll down his white face.

"You're a loser, Ed! Look atcha! You're a no good father! You read meters for Christ sake! What kind of job is that for a man? What kinda role model are you for our sons? You're disgusting and a loser. Sleep on the couch! I can't stand the smell of you! You're so full of crap that I can smell it!"

His ex's insults haunted and taunted him. When the words were at their full power he'd reach for the psyllium, dissolve it in the orange juice and gulp it down. It cleaned him out like nothing else. When the words refused to vacate his mind he'd go to the local swimming pool and sit for hours in the sauna and in his mind. Sweating cleansed him further. He'd lift his arms and sniff until he felt clean.

His clowning turned out to be a success. His website showed him busy for months. He'd race home after reading meters all day and, with much gusto, do his makeup and put on his costume. He always grabbed a handful of balloons for the party kids and packed along his air pump. He'd leave his apartment whistling, and for the enjoyment of Marjorie, the senior who always poked a head out of her apartment when she heard his door shut, skip a little jump in his bright, red, oversized shoes.

But as time went on, Ed became lonely. He'd leave his gigs feeling empty after being around happy, giggling children and their parents. And he missed the intimacy of a woman. One night after a full day's work he found himself sculpting lewd balloons. At first it was just woman's bosoms, but it soon progressed to male reproductive organs. He worked diligently, nightly, trying to perfect the final product. At last he did, and felt compelled to offer the work to a cute blond who served him coffee at the Starbucks drive-thru on his way to weekend gigs. He was too shy to ask anyone out and still felt like 'a stinking loser'. He thought this might be a way to let her know he was interested.

Dressed in costume with full makeup, he inched his red 'smart car' to the takeout window.

"Hi Clown Man. On your way to work?" she giggled as she typically did when he pulled up.

"Yes, I am. I have a special balloon for you. Here..." he reached in the back seat and pulled out the lewd balloon he made special for her that morning. It was his best work he thought. A work of art. It was, without a doubt, an erect penis and testicles.

"Oh!" She passed him the coffee and her hand reached out. "What is it? Oh dear..." she blushed and turned away.

He moved forward in the 'smart car', glancing into his rear view mirror.

A smile brightened his sad clown face.

Gangle

by Bruce Reisner

(Mature: some coarse language)

I'm just dying my hair to black. It's a dollar job, buck a pop at the store, and it's soaking into my head right now like uranium. But it really, really helps to keep it dark on top. But there is a problem.

Earlier today I tested my new electric power assist bicycle on a long run. Mission sucked, it was as strenuous as riding a road bike the same distance. Laws of physics, blow me. As soon as I got my wind back for the trip, I looked in the mirror, saw how under-the-bridge my hair looked, and went for my hair dye pack like a spawning salmon.

The skull cap of sludge is turning colder, but I don't put that in front of my dog pack of misery. Just a second ago, I got an excruciating spasm. I'm in screaming pain, and the shit on top of my head, last I checked the mirror, has me looking like an undesirable. I am going to have to amble to the kitchen sink, to hose the shit out of my hair. Will soon be hiking like the Hunchback, swearing and screaming. Can't fucking wait.

I got another ten minutes before the hose, so here's the special thing that happened on the bike trip. Most of the way home, the battery was showing near discharged. The bike weighs 75 badly placed pounds, hills here are steep, spires you might say. To discharge completely would hurt. Like now.

A few blocks from home, working the last volts the battery liked to donate, like corporate America, I decided to rest near the high rise. There's a double lot where two crack houses used to compete like Sears and Monkey Wards. The demolition squad left some of the cinder blocks from the basements, providing a cozy cold corner—minus the rest of the room—to scrooch up in. Corners were made for cowering. There I was, perfect.

This gangle of cut and dragged morning glory vines tied the room together, like a tall house plant. It looked more like hybrid tumbleweed with a crown of thorns. This area has a lot of Catholics, so you get that sort of effect, in shit that blows in and out of here. My cinder block corner had an open view of the first floor of the highrise, beehive of dysfunction and ease, illness and freedom from hard labor.

The words, "Hi there, hi there," started flying like hawks and doves in the air. At first I tried to ignore it, since I wasn't aware I was being spoken to. I'm good about cleaning my plate when you have me over for dinner—might even fold the napkin. Whatever.

You don't go looking to see who it is that's talking, unless you know them, and their doe eyes are meeting yours, absent of malice. Otherwise, you pretend people aren't there.

"Hi there" kept flapping its blowzy, heather wings. The flesh is weak. I started to look around.

"Look up higher," she said.

First I looked at the fifth floor of the highrise, and its usual row of vacant unseasoned concrete balconies. I looked at my bike like it was half guilty for what was happening. It's fucking near time to rinse the liquid plutonium gel that will soon fix my repulsive gray hair. Presto change-o, it will be black. I might look young again when this is over.

On the seventh floor, when the moon is in the seventh house...As soon as I looked up there, she entered my life with all the familiarity that modern times lack. I'm a lucky piece of shit with a not too successful electric bike.

A huge woman in a night gown was talking to me from on high. Shit like this happened in the Bible, but things were more substantive in those days.

She seemed to like me. And Mercury aligns with Mars. This was not the sort of woman that gives me the big hard one. The batteries 'down there' have been running lower than in years past, but there is still a supply of juice. The visage above didn't help. But damn it all, she was friendly.

The little bell on my clock spring timer just went 'ding,' and I must get this shit out of my hair, so I am going to leave off at how I conversed with the huge woman, she waving her arms in the air like a big bird, her too transparent nightie doing a dance to the bounding flesh. We conversed, about nothing but the weather, "fine as could be asked for," and maybe how 'sweet it is' to have such a fine resting spot right where I was. She was right, I had my own corner of a demolished basement to hang in until both legs got half back to normal. Damn, like the ending in The Yearling.

Maybe it's a hamstring. Something cord-like and imperative—feels like it is tearing loose from the trailer hitch nearest my ass. This bullshit has to mean something, or else another thing would have happened. I know per usual that after the hair dye rinses out, the skin on my forehead and face will have embarrassing stains that take about a day or two to wear off.

View From the Food Court
by Sheila Cano

Perched by the window two stories above the parking lot, I work at ingesting a week's worth of sodium content in one Thai take-out lunch. My vantage point yields a panoramic view of two hundred cars below, the Skytrain above, and highrise apartment buildings in the middle distance. The horizon is a hazy silhouette of more highrises and tall evergreen trees.

In the absence of reading material, I amuse myself counting all the red and blue cars, little bits of matchbox colour among the sea of drab black, gray and silver. I see the ones who lurk, cruising slowly, looking for the back-up lights of a vehicle about to pull out of a space. Sometimes there is a conflict: two lurkers vying for the same space. One puts on the turn signal to indicate, "I saw it first." The other one edges past, and I can almost feel the driver's annoyance from way up here above the lot.

I survey the urban landscape, with its noise of tires on wet pavement mimicking the swish of a stream, the car horns reminiscent of the alarm calls of birds. If all the people who arrived in cars stood on the expanse of asphalt, they would take

106

up only one lane of parking spaces. At the end of a row, a little plot of bushes represents the developer's afterthought about including "nature" in the plan.

The echo chamber of the food court reverberates with the hollow sounds of fellow foragers who have each selected their meal from one of the dozen outlets. An occasional piercing scream from a toddler, or a rasping laugh from a tobacco-ravaged throat, punctuates the hub-bub. The metal chair legs scrape harshly on the tile floor, an irritating noise obviously not considered by the interior design firm.

The Skytrain station is one of the better looking ones, an elongated oval bubble made up of panes of blue-green glass. It looks futuristic, a nod to the sci-fi vision of a city of tall buildings connected by elevated transit routes. All that's missing are the little personal aircraft floating above the scene. I finish my spicy lunch, toss the Styrofoam plate into the garbage, which will eventually end up in some landfill in Washington State. I make my way back to my car, freeing up a space for the big black SUV waiting impatiently for me to leave.

Sidelines

by Adrienne S Moody

(Mature: some coarse language)

She is 86 years old and she does look it. She moves slowly and often gets stuck, frozen like a computer with too many commands that simply stops. Humiliation is what she feels when she's taken to the washroom that she shares with another elderly woman, to receive fresh ***Depends***.

"Leave me alone, you miserable prick!" is her usual response, but she reluctantly gives in with her head hanging in submission.

Her husband passed three years ago. He lived in the same facility but up on the third floor where the Alzheimer's patients are kept under lock and key. She'd visit him regularly at first, but it depressed her so, to see him once so bright and strong, pushing an empty food cart up and down the hallways. She grieved for him, but knew he was no longer suffering.

Months after the memorial, when she settled back into her room after an outing, she sat down on her bed and felt something under her bottom. She shrieked in surprise and stood abruptly for a woman of her age and disability. She pulled out the remote control and smiled.

"I thought for a minute it was my Vincey, but then I remembered he's dead!"

She isolates herself from the rest of the residents living there. No one meets her higher level of thinking, so she stays in her room watching programs like CSI, hockey, baseball and her favorite, tennis. She was a pro tennis player in her prime.

There are mementos from Australia, her homeland, and she often thinks of the outback and the hot sun. Her son still lives there and sends her flowers on Mother's Day, Christmas and her birthday.

She dreams of going back home. Often, when she finishes lunch and the three ladies at her table nod off, she glances out the window and remembers running the courts, and the sound of her racket acing a shot.

Judea Worthy
by M Dawn Thacker

Judy Worthy spends her time preaching. She used to call
herself Judy, however she's become "Minister Judea". She
attended divinity school in someone's basement, was ordained by
the church, and now doesn't let anyone forget it, especially the
homeless.

She's a street preacher, selling the Lord like a dealer in front
of the Chapman IGA on Locust Avenue. Sunday morning, people
walk past, buying beer, eggs, and cigarettes. Some are dressed for
church in the building under the steeple on Main Street. Others
are still dressed for bed. Minister Judea watches and searches for
the lost. She knows them by the look in their eye, the tangles in
their hair—by the stagger in their step.

"Come to the Lord," she yells from behind her black book.
"Find Him now, before it's too late. Give up your life of
iniquity."

She is not familiar with the concept of personal space. The
title of 'Minister' gives her certain privileges, like pointing a
finger to heaven—or at someone—slamming a fist on her Bible,

or slinging spit at the faces of her congregation. She preaches up close and personal.

Most people look away. Their eyes channel surf to the cars in the parking lot, the trees in the distance, or to their shopping bags of bread and wine.

"You will look at me and hear the word," she calls to individuals, straining her voice and the tendons in her neck.

One disheveled man in a motorized scooter approaches.

"My name's John," he says. "I want to be healed." He allows her to lay hands on his damaged legs, hoping for God's miracle.

Minister Judea prays over him, calling God to come to the parking lot of the grocery store and purchase this man's sin. She pleads, "John, you must confess. You are a sinner. You do not deserve God's grace and mercy—no one does. He will give it to you, though, if you believe."

John looks up at her. He's wanted someone to help him count sins for a long time.

"Yes," he vows.

"Come to this man, oh Lord. Show him the way. Fill him with your presence and make him whole." Her voice shakes with

111

a spirit. She lifts her eyes to the sky then raises her hands. John watches and waits.

The city beat cop walks near, his fingers wrapped around the handle of the billy club hanging from his belt.

"You need to move along now," the officer announces to Minister Judea. "This is private property."

John scowls, his miracle interrupted.

Minister Judea shouts, "I am the way and the truth and the life. No one comes to the Father except through me."

The sermon has ended. She closes her book, turns her back, and walks away.

Wind whips a weekly sales flier around the parking lot. It announces: *Easter Savings at Your Neighborhood IGA.*

Class Identity
by Sarah Scott

I wander yellow concrete halls in a stupor, but never disengaged. Noticing the sideways glances of entwined lovers, the stains on the floors from I don't know what, and the stooping shoulders, heavy-laden frames of people, milling from class to class. I see the guy in front of me stare at the black girl's ass and hear his friends snicker. I cringe. Professors drag themselves to another room to drone on as they did the hour before, their monotone voices reverberating off blank stares and falling on deaf ears. I groan and take my seat, another faceless grade on the books. Identity is lost in a place like this, or perhaps it's stolen away by the endless hours of pouring over texts, revising essays, and crunching numbers—the balance of the days' tasks makes my head spin. Class begins.

Fancy Pants

by Gaboo

Fancy pants
seen struttin' and posin, nosin' and moseyin'.
Fancy pants
big fat hat, shine sham, rattle trap
slippery slap finger rings string-a-long diamonds and bling
waggin' ragtag entourage of monkey swag
with instantaneous superficial cranial consumption business
on a double wide bow-rider painted in eye-horn colors.
Fancy pants
makes me rant, all your "Ooh, I want this. Don't say that I can't."
Well, rust and mildew will last longer than you,
Fancy pants.

The Grand Pumstuffing of
Significance and Windeblough
by Gaboo

Cavalier Significance
Ponced preening riddlybows,
"Wilt yea handy me 'o pampoustool,
Fair Thutlass Windeblough?"

"On flouster, goodly ploon."
And so thus they whenced flouted–
Cardiganly cumperstowed,
Pumstuffing pip exposed!

Desperate farling, hardly!
"Smartly!" Thutlass winced entow.
Significance waned nor wavered not,
Lest all winds up on show.

Cavalier dimmed tippy.
Thutlass slacked a node,
"Fell doupkist, dearing granisludes."
"Fell donkdip, Windeblough!"

The Corner of Angus and Emmet
by M Dawn Thacker

(Mature: some coarse language)

The locals roll up their windows and stare straight ahead. Most ignore her presence. Some taunt or curse her. Catherine sits in a wheelchair on the corner of Angus and Emmet, on the same side of the street as the Kentucky Fried Chicken. She parks exactly fifteen feet from the bus stop, right there at the traffic light. In summer, she wears a cotton duster. In winter, she wears a cotton duster.

Catherine rolls out early on Tuesday morning, half a bucket of Saturday's popcorn secured in her lap by a bungee cord stretched across the armrests of her wheelchair. There's a hill just at the end of Angus and she needs both hands to hold back the wheelchair from careening into southbound traffic. Emmet is a busy highway. She has mastered the incline that leads to the sidewalk where she sits. Maneuvering is only difficult when someone at the beauty shop remembers to turn on the sprinklers the night before and the grass is wet. Even if she struggles, no one helps her.

Traffic picks up about 7:15. Catherine allows herself fifteen minutes to park and settle. She adjusts her seating and the distance from the curb to the exact inch. The 6:55 Blue Line bus heading downtown is on time. Catherine smiles. She hates it when the bus is late and interrupts her start time. Her schedule dictates she man her station Tuesday, Thursday and Saturday from 7:00 a.m. sharp until 2:30 in the afternoon. She takes a break, but it's never during lunch hour. The traffic is heavy then. She would miss opportunities. The movie theater manager allows her to use the bathroom, because she buys an extra large tub of popcorn and sometimes a drink, if it's hot. She never buys a ticket, only refreshments. The cost is budgeted into her monthly expenses. Her disability check comes a few days after the third of the month, because her birthday is on the third of October.

She watches and waits for the first red light after 7:00. The light is green. She waits. It turns yellow and she counts the five seconds until red. Bingo. Sitting before her is a blue station wagon. She reaches into the tub and takes out one piece of popcorn, holding it between her thumb and index finger. She closes one eye, aims, and throws the kernel at the passenger window of the car. She repeats this action until she hits the center of the window or until the light turns green. Sometimes the window is open and she scores points. When she misses her mark, she curses loudly starting with "Damn!" If she misses

117

again, "Double Damn!" Again, "Triple Damn!" Then, on to, "Son of a Bitch!" And on those days when the wind is blowing, she sometimes finishes with a resounding, "Fuck!"

The locals know her. Tourists don't. At 10:35, a red BMW is the target. The passenger is a boy. His father is driving. Catherine aims and hits her mark. The electric window slides down.

"Stop that!" the man says.

Catherine aims again, for points this time. She throws and misses.

"Damn!" she says.

"Hey," the man yells, "what's wrong with you?"

She aims again, throws, no points. "Double Damn!" she says.

"Lady, shut up and stop it," the man yells, his face turning red. "Can't you see a kid's in here?"

The wind picks up. Catherine aims again, throws and misses.

"Triple Damn!" she says.

The man turns on his flashers, puts the car in park, and gets out. He stomps to the sidewalk and yells, "You crazy old bat. What kind of example are you setting for children? Don't you have anything better to do?" He picks up her bucket of popcorn and dumps it on the sidewalk, slamming the empty tub back into Catherine's lap.

"Son of a Bitch!" Catherine says, as the man stomps back to his car and peels off. She turns her wheelchair around and pushes up the hill to the movie theater. It opens every day at 11:00. She enters the door with the empty bucket, a full bladder and $4.00 in crumpled bills. If she hurries, she can make it back down the hill before the lunchtime rush.

Night Ride

by Sheila Cano

On a downtown Friday night, I managed to get a seat before the bus filled up with people heading home to the suburbs. The only passenger close to my age was a short man dressed in jeans and a tweed jacket, a fedora on his head. His small facial features reminded me of a lemur, as he glanced around nervously before starting a conversation with the young man sitting next to him. I thought he might be a retired jockey. The rest of the bus riders were young, mostly in their twenties, exhaling alcohol fumes into the air.

The bus lurched forward from the last stop before the causeway through the park, throwing some off balance as they clung to the overhead straps. One guy staggered, and others caught him before he fell down.

"Oh, man, he's really drunk," said a blonde woman wearing knee-high black boots and a leather jacket with too many zippers.

"Someone tell the bus driver," her companion said. The blonde worked her way up to the front, squeezing past other wobbly folks, and let the driver know he had some damaged cargo on board. Not that there was a lot he could do about it, other than hope the guy didn't throw up.

"This guy needs to sit down," another woman said. Two people got up, and helped the drunken one lie down across the seats, his legs hanging off the end into the aisle. He passed out.

The driver dimmed the interior lights as we came to the bridge. Eerie little rectangles of light glowed here and there in the darkness as people logged onto their PDAs and cell phones. One girl's device was sheathed in a pink plastic case. She alternately punched the mini-keypad and took bites from a gooey-looking piece of cake, while her friend peered over to look at the screen. They were both dressed in dated Hello Kitty couture, pastel pink and white hoodies and short, pleated skirts. Other riders had little cords dangling from their ears, tinny noises issuing from their mp3 players.

I looked out the window at the city lights sparkling over the water. The young woman in the seat next to mine tilted her glowing screen slightly away from me, and I sensed her discomfort at my head being turned towards her. Perhaps she thought I was snooping, which I might have done except the display was so small there's no way I could have figured out what she was watching. Each person seemed to be in their own little bubble, sheltered from human interaction by way of their electronic gadgets.

We arrived at the first stop on the North Shore, and several people got off. The guy who passed out woke up, and tried to stand up.

"Whoa, careful," said the blonde in the zippered jacket. She grabbed his arm to steady him.

"Driver, can you wait a bit? He's having trouble getting up."

Two people held him and walked him off the bus.

"OK, he made it. Man, was he ever ripped."

Rarely do I ride the buses. As we neared my stop, I reflected upon my reactions to the experience. Being around so many people in a small space, I understand why each person turns to their electronic toys to shut out the world. Secure in my car, listening to CDs, I am removed from contact with the crowd. Yet this night, strangers responded to care for the one who was vulnerable. I stepped off the bus and inhaled a deep breath of fresh night air, and walked briskly to my apartment building. Once inside, I turned on the lights, took off my jacket and then booted up the computer.

Read This Please

Volume 1 Edition 3 - Father, Where art thou?

June 16, 2010

In this edition, we celebrated the patriarchs of the family, our fathers on their special day.

My Pa

by Sheila Cano

a papoose on his mother's back
staring up at the sun while she picked fruit
a farm worker as a child in the central valley
a young man in the thirties
a sailor around the horn
a translator for the WPA writers project
he helped build San Francisco
a longshoreman on the docks
a pile driver for the Nimitz freeway
the Embarcadero and so many buildings
a carpenter until retirement
hands the size of dinner plates
his neck broken from a falling beam
discs fused in his back
fifty years of pain
glaucoma from sun damage
stone deaf from no ear protection

some Saturdays we went to the toy store
he bought me two comic books

124

a plastic horse for my birthday
a model car kit
use the glue outside he said
don't breathe it in

he loved birds creatures and plants
a closet botanist
we called him the professor
he gave me binoculars when I was seventeen
a bird book and a plant guide
I still have them
leather strap torn
book bindings worn

he taught me how to use his tools
how to hammer nails
how to saw
measure twice cut once
yet he told me not to work with my hands
to study and become educated
use my mind not my body
when I was thirty six I built a stairway
I have his sawdust in my blood

at ninety his last project
fixing the deck

up on a fifteen foot ladder

he let me spot him

hand him the tools

eighty degree sunshine

no water bottle

my stepmother said

you are the only one he ever let help him

the only one he ever let drive his Camaro

he sleeps now

ashes under the Mexican lime tree

in the backyard

On Safari

by Adrienne S Moody

(Mature: some coarse language)

"My father was the superintendent of an old-age institution for men. This was back in the days where they segregated the men from the women. He was in charge of approximately 150 men and a staff of 80. We lived in a section off from the facility but shared one wall. I remember an old-timer named Wallace Hilldebrandt. He loved to eavesdrop on our family and could often be found with his ear to the common wall. There he'd be sitting slumped in his wheelchair, the side of his face pressed to the institutional green wall and eyes staring off into space. My brother and me would pound on it from time to time from the other side, or open the door mere feet from where he'd be sitting and yell, 'Did ya hear that, Wallace Hilldebrandt?' That would scare the crap out of the old goat. Oh yeah, we had some good times.

The city jail was next door and hand-picked prisoners in their black and whites would tend to the gardens around the joint. I figured we were lucky, my brother and I, to live in such a sprawling home. Stories of goings on at either facility would be

127

recanted at dinnertime and a few of the tales would curl your hair. We saw our share of stiffies, let me tell you.

I swear one time, running down the halls, I turned a corner and went into the room we were forbidden to enter. I saw one such stiff laid out on a table and damned if he didn't suddenly sit straight up. My Father said nerves will do that to a corpse.

My brother Samuel and I would often be woken in the middle of the night with my father shining a flashlight into our faces. He'd say, 'We're going on a safari, boys. Are you up for an adventure tonight, or are you sissies and gotta get your beauty rest?' he'd say or something like that. We just jumped into our shoes and pulled a coat over our pj's and raced to the waiting car.

'Where we goin' tonight, Pa?' I'd ask excitedly.

We would climb into the front and I would fumble with the radio dials. Static and rock-and-roll set the mood for the upcoming adventure. My father liked to roam the streets in the middle of the night and he often found something to show us that had a lesson tied to it. Seldom did we come home without something to think about. One time the streets and bars were so quiet that he did something he'd never done. He wheeled us down a country road to the City Pound.

"Why are we here, Pa?" Samuel asked.

128

Pa said nothing, just shut the ignition off and we listened. The sound of cats and dogs making their racket filled the air. Barking and yelping and cats meowing...it was the saddest sound I'd ever heard. Most of the time he'd find something for us to see that we'd never seen before. He liked to park outside mansions and make us guess how many kids lived there, what their lives were like. Then before he drove us home he'd be sure to pass by the slum like a warning. I'll never forget the broken windows and garbage and beat up cars on the lawn. I was always happy to get home after a safari like that one."

Gordon looked down at his shoes and spent twenty or so seconds in deep thought. Someone in the third row cleared their throat.

"One Halloween night when I just turned 16, he pulled in front of the Central Hotel. We sat watching people leave the bar into the darkness, stumbling and some calling out incoherently. Then we saw two natives exit with their arms around each other trying not to fall. That's when we saw the cops come out from nowhere and at first they just talked to them.

Then they pushed them around and without any reason that we could see, they began to punch and kick them once they dropped to the ground.

129

'What's goin' on, Pa?' I whispered.

'Just watch,' he said.

"We did and I never seen such a beating. When I looked away, my father noticed and ordered me to watch. Once the cops left and disappeared around the corner, he started up the car and we drove slowly away without our headlights on. I don't know what the lesson was with that one. Was it to show us what can happen if we drink too much, or what happens if you're native in our city, or, the one I decided on, don't drink in that bar and I never did.

Gordon stopped talking to sip some water. He pulled a napkin from his pocket and wiped his forehead.

"I tell people I had a great childhood. I got no complaints. But that night stayed with me, man. We could have done something, but we didn't. We watched and I remember looking at my father's face as we passed under the streetlights but I couldn't read him. Anyway, the story goes on. The two natives didn't make it. They did find the cops who beat them to death and they were given really light sentences. I've been carrying this for 26 years now.

So if I can name something that got me drinking it'd be that. That night changed me and I can't forgive myself for not trying to stop what was happening right in front of me. I get in such a state on the anniversary date, Halloween, and this is the first Halloween I've been sober, so that's why I'm here and thanks for listening."

Gordon stepped down off the small stage of the community center and sat down in the front row. He spent the rest of the evening with his wife and 12 year old son. They lived on a block with few young children, so their evening was interrupted only a few times with trick-or-treaters at the door eagerly holding out Halloween bags.

He had trouble sleeping that night and just after midnight he threw the covers off, dressed himself quietly.

"Please don't go out, Gordon. Are you going to take Charles again on that silly safari thing you do?" his wife sat up in bed scratching her head sleepily.

"Go to sleep. We won't be long. A drive will calm me and help me sleep."

In his son's darkened bedroom he shined a flashlight into his sleeping face.

"Son, it's safari night. C'mon, get dressed and I'll meet you in the car."

As he waited outside with the motor running, he thought of all the times he dragged his son out of bed half-tanked and drove aimlessly around the city, the same city he grew up in. Gordon knew his outings, safaris, never seemed to hold the excitement and the provoking of thought that his father seemed always capable of bringing about. He felt that since he quit drinking, they were at least talking and getting to know each other without the booze.

"Where we going, Dad?" Charles climbed into the front seat and clipped his seat belt on. He was about to plug himself into his mp3, but his father protested.

"C'mon, tune into me, okay?"

"Borrrring..."

He found himself heading downtown and decided to swing by the Central Hotel. There had been a few renovations in the past decade or so, but it was still a down-and-outer kind of bar.

"Where we goin', Dad?"

"Let's check out skid row."

"Why not hooker street?"

"Some other time. Let's see what trouble is going on down at the Central."

He pulled to a stop across from the blinking neon sign and turned the engine off. It was now nearly one a.m. and a wind picked leaves up off the road and sidewalk and moved them along; the scuttling sound caused goose bumps along Gordon's arms. Like fingernails along a chalkboard, he thought. Suddenly the doors swung open and two men swaggered out, one wrapped his arm around the other's shoulders in an effort, it seemed, not to fall.

They were natives and although it couldn't be, looked very much like the two he witnessed as a young man. Two cops appeared suddenly and they began to jostle them, just as what happened before. The violence escalated into punching and the sound of the male moans could be heard. The two were on the ground and the uniformed officers began to kick at them, their heads and abdomen. It couldn't be, but he knew it was, the same four playing out the same scenario as he witnessed years before.

"What the fuck, Dad? Aren't you gonna do something?" Charles was near tears.

"Just watch," he whispered back to his son.

133

Hottest Day of the Year

by Gaboo

Took my boy for a ride on a train.
Chance to see the city again.
Lot's of motion, commotion,
lot's of grime and grit—
gotta tell him where to walk
and how to find a clean place to sit.

And there's some junkie yelling at us for laughing.
Seems there's only room here for straight up types doing nothing.
It's got its lights and its horns,
and that big city charm,
but my boy still sees things for value
and not what can harm.

That's what we did
on the hottest day of the year.

My boy, he sees the store where Chris Cringle pays his visits.
He reminds me too, like it's something I should miss.
We see that lady
selling her hot cross buns.

My boy gets his with lots of sauce,
and I get mine with none.

That's what we did
on the hottest day of the year.

You know they gotta lot of stars out
on the hottest day of the year.
And late night TV talks about everybody's fears.
I see my boy lying in his bed;
he's got all of his dreams rolling through his head.

That's what we did
on the hottest day of the year.

Red Rose Valley
by Casimirr Rexregys

The weekend before camping in Red Rose Valley, Casi was invited to a dinner gathering with the family of his classmate, John. John's father was the top man in the Royal Observatory, an extremely learned professional and a body builder, weighing two hundred and seventy pounds, and standing six feet, four inches. John's mother was a petite lady, with the same light brown eyes and hair as John and his younger sister. John and his sister were physically smaller than average kids.

The food was good, and after desert, John's mother brought up a question on innateness. It was the wrong idea, trying to create a 'like father, like son' topic around the table, and an improper way to repair the relationship of John and his father. John failed all his exams, skipped school, and spent all his free time with a girl whose father was an organized crime boss. There was no way to convince John's father that bad things began within the family. Casi and John were not interested in such pointless debate. Although Casi did not see much of his own father—they repelled each other in many ways—Casi felt his father was the only hero in his heart.

136

Mr. McCain was not a popular leader among his troop of Catholic Scouts; he was known to wander off when there were outdoor activities. Now leading a patrol of eight scouts into Red Rose Valley for their first Patrol Camp, McCain disappeared into the woods after a sudden drop in temperature and change in the wind. While the other scouts were preparing the campsite, Casi and his friend John hiked off to find paths through unexplored territory.

"Down the creek," Casi said, "One of us has to go first."

"You first," John stated.

"Wait," Casi hesitated.

"What?"

"Keep your position—look over the top of my beret," Casi uttered in a low voice when using his head to point, while blocking John's view from something directly ahead.

"Run," John exclaimed, "Casi RUN!"

A torrent swept the valley as they reached camp. There was no sign of Leader McCain and the scouts began digging a ditch surrounding the collapsible tent. They rotated positions, finishing the trench before nightfall and redirecting rain water away from the clothes, sleeping bags and gear stowed inside.

Heavy rain poured over the tent, while eight tenderfoot scouts of more or less the same age, and from the same private school, tugged on sleeping bags in the dark. Everyone was soaked and hungry. Their duty was to camp for one night before being promoted to Second Class Scouts. McCain chose the Red Rose Valley site at the School Master's request, a small valley by the seaside within a noted residential area for the rich and famous of the island. The School Master's intent was to shelter students from public school rough kids at conventional campsites. Now their leader had either abandoned the children or was lost.

"We saw a corpse with maggots," Casi said casually after everyone settled down, "hung on the tree half way down the creek."

This was Casi's usual practice, to avoid alarming the other kids who may never have seen anything so scary. The patrol was comprised of well-off youth; most of them experiencing their first time out in the wild.

Before anyone responded to Casi's statement, a few scouts screamed—a tall, human figure appeared at the entrance of the tent.

138

"Father?" Casi uttered lightly from the far end.

"Don't get up," Mr. Rexregys gave a steaming, hot bag to the nearest scout and spoke in an empowered voice with authority, "This should be enough for all of you."

"Thanks, Mr. Rexregys," The scouts responded in unison.

"No worry," Mr. Rexregys smiled and said, "Good night and sleep well."

"Good Night, Mr. Rexregys,"

Hours earlier, Mr. Rexregys sat unaware that his chauffeur, Paul, was driving the patriarch to see his son, Casi. Paul was once the head of the Syndicate street gang. Paul had tired of those rough days; his men betrayed him, and his daughter hung out with a rich kid. Paul now made a decent living in working for Mr. Rexregys, who hired the ex-gangster and listened to his life stories. Paul had fought a life saving battle to protect Mr. Rexregys from a distressed person in High Street, where they first met. Months later, with Mr. Rexregys' help and words of advice, Paul's wife and family owned a line of legitimate music stores, avoiding pirated material.

"Red Rose Valley," Mr. Rexregys spoke, "What does this valley mean to you, Paul?"

"If not because of you, Mr. Rexregys," Paul replied, "I might hang myself there."

"Must have a good reason for suicide," Mr. Rexregys said, "Remember, you once said suicide is for those who suffer from cowardice."

"Yes," Paul sighed, "that was how you saved my life—you gave me a second chance to take better care of myself."

"Every person has only two chances," Mr. Rexregys said, "You did not waste any."

"That valley is a perfect hideaway," Paul said, "There are pirate tunnels and passageways, but the curse is—a place of no return for those who are cursed."

Paul continued, "Casi found one of the tunnels up in the peak a year ago, his hideout ever since, and he has followers."

"These followers will disappoint or betray him one day," Paul carried on, "not when you are still alive."

"Tell me more," Mr. Rexregys said coldly.

"Casi will work hard on your dreams and wishes," Paul said, "Your wife will not—your other sons will not."

Mr. Rexregys and Paul were sitting in silence when the car arrived next to a path leading into Red Rose Valley.

"These hot buns are enough for all the kids," Paul said, returning from the boot and handing over a curved, European umbrella designed for a single person.

Many years later, Casi's father died a sudden death. On his death bed, Casi was the only son who listened to his last words, when all others were suffering from flu in wards throughout the private hospital.

In a walk-in security room, Casi deciphered his father's written works word for word, and understood every unfinished line. Casi did not know how to cry, but he remembered the rainy night when his father came through the torrent with enough hot buns for everybody.

Ashes to Dust

by Adrienne S Moody

I've written a few good ghost stories in my life, but they were fiction. The best story of all is one that is true. Isn't that usually the case? If you have a few moments, let me tell you of the time that I witnessed the actions of a ghost. My best friend exclaimed upon hearing this story, "That's a poltergeist!" to which I admonished her with, "My father is certainly not that!" But, I am ahead of myself.

My father died a dreadful death. Lung cancer and emphysema slowly choked the air from him and he drowned in his own fluids. I flew home every month for nearly a year to visit and try to help. These visits filled me with anguish and I would go home and recuperate, preparing myself for the next and tried not to think of the inevitable. His death was the first in our family and we all suffered in our own way. Denial proved to be an effective defense for most of us. I was the closest to him. When my sister called me with the news that he had lung cancer, I knew without her telling me that it was terminal. No one could really say how long he would last, but obviously his lease on life was short.

142

For that first month of knowing my father was dying, I would wake in the middle of the night with my heart racing and at first I couldn't figure out what was wrong in my life. And then the realization that it was him, he would soon be dead, drew my knees to my chest and I tried to breathe around what felt like a knife in my ribcage. My father had been a drinker most of his adult life and his behavior towards his children was, without a doubt, emotionally and physically abusive.

When he quit drinking cold turkey ten years before he died, I witnessed a side to him that his drinking hid. I will remember the simple moments like sitting at the kitchen table with him and sharing the newspaper. He'd point out something amusing to me and we'd smirk like conspirators. My mother indulged us by leaving us be, clearing her throat, pushing her spectacles higher up on her nose, studying her crossword. Oh, he still could be miserable and make us jump with ugly words when we didn't answer quick enough, or agree with him, but he was now malleable.

At the border crossing one time, I passed my ID to the border guard and when he asked me where we had been in the States, I answered wrong. To be honest, I felt my father glaring at me from the passenger seat and my mind went blank. He could rattle me with just a glance.

"That's not right! We were in Bellingham!" his voice spit the words out in a snarl.

"It's okay, Dad..." I turned to him pleading him with my eyes to 'not do this, not now..'

I turned back to the guard. He caught it all and smiled kindly at me and passed my ID back. My father would be dead two weeks later. It was obvious to anyone looking at him that he was deathly ill, the skin stretched across his cheek bones, gaunt, his gray skin tone.

When he disengaged himself from the oxygen tank to light a cigarette, he looked like a smoking ghost. But, we had those quiet, calm moments that I will remember. He loved nature as I do and this was our bond. We watched David Suzuki together and I nodded my head in agreement when he would say, "Now, that man should be Prime Minister."

And we played blackjack together at the local casino. This was a new activity that we began after his diagnosis. My mother gave us one hour, exactly, to go and be back. My father put his watch on the counter and motioned to the dealer to deal us in. I was on a winning streak. I seemed to know instinctively when to hold and when to draw. I couldn't lose. I left with cash in my pocket and my father would desperately plug the slot machines with quarters on the way out. His luck had run out.

My brother closest to me in age envied this new found bond I had with him and asked my mother why I seemed to have such a good relationship with him. She answered with the truth which was, "She works at it." I wouldn't walk away when he ranted. I stayed and waited till the angry wave passed. And it would, pass.

When he berated me for answering wrong during his favorite game, Trivial Pursuit, he looked puzzled when I did not respond to his insults. I let him finish and then calmly passed the dice. Slowly, his armor began to chip away. A week before his death I made an error in my departure time. I arrived at the airport only to find I missed my flight. I knew my dad drove to the airport to pick me up. I knew he was very sick but insisted stubbornly he wanted to do this. And now I missed my flight and had to wait for the next one two hours later. I couldn't get hold of him as he didn't have such a thing as a cell phone.

When I finally arrived and searched the crowd for someone from my family, my brother came up behind me, startled me and proceeded to scold me for my having caused dad great distress by driving all that way for nothing.

"He is so stressed out, Adrienne, he barely could make it home!"

I couldn't apologize enough. During that last visit I took him to his last doctor's appointment where his chest was x-rayed one more time. I watched as he feebly stood in front of that cold machine, this man who used to be an athlete, who could beat his sons at any sport they cared to challenge him with. I watched him and knew he faced defeat for the first time. I buttoned up his shirt afterward and he spoke to me.

"I know they can't do anything more to help me. What is mom going to do when I'm gone?" and for the first time ever, I saw my father cry.

"I'll look after her, dad. We'll all look after her. Don't worry. I promise," and he stopped crying.

He believed me. That was the last time I saw him alive. My sister called on a Friday and told me that he was admitted into Palliative Care at the hospital and likely would not live more than a couple of days. I, as well as the rest of my siblings, living scatted across North America, booked our flights home.

My flight departed at 7:00 AM Saturday morning. I asked my partner, Dan, to please set his clock for 4:00 AM and to wake me promptly. I could not miss this flight. I was to be the first to arrive and my mother needed me there. I vowed to keep my promise. I slept on the fold out couch in the living room which was next to the kitchen. Dan slept in our bedroom at the other end of the house which was separated by two doors and a back entryway.

At midnight the dreaded call came in that he passed away. My brother's voice sounded...scared. I felt strangely peaceful and hung up the phone and told Dan I was fine, just please go back to bed, let me sleep and don't sleep in past the alarm. I slept soundly. At precisely 4:00 AM he shook my shoulder gently. I sipped hot coffee at the kitchen table. Dan sat facing me staring intently into my eyes.

"What?" I finally asked.

He cleared his throat.

"Your dad was here last night," he finally spoke in a whisper. He looked excited.

"Shut up! Don't say things like that, Dan." I felt a chill travel down my spine. I stood and held my hand out to halt him. "I don't want to hear this."

I left the room and dressed. I re-entered the kitchen with my suitcase. I sat back down.

"Okay, tell me."

"He was here, Adrienne. At about 3:45 AM I heard all this crashing in the kitchen. Cupboards banging shut, drawers slamming. I thought you were angry that I didn't get you up. I yelled out, 'Okay, I'll get up!' I went into the kitchen and there's no one there. I checked on you and you were sound asleep. He was here, Adrienne. How could you not hear that racket?"

I passed the stewardess my ticket and found my seat. Once in the air and the seat belt light went out, I unbuckled and settled in, wrapping my coat around me. I looked out the window at nothing. Darkness. I felt warmth. I can't describe it any better than that. I knew it was him. He made damn sure his daughter caught that flight and would be there for his wife, my mother, during this time. The initial prickly fear that I felt upon hearing Dan's recounting of the event, was replaced by this strange warmth. I felt him around me for days afterward. He faced his death with such courage and then showed me that death is not so final, not in the way we think. It was one of his final gifts from him to me.

Too Late

by M Dawn Thacker

We were late. We'd stayed at the park too long. The sun wasn't hot anymore. The slide didn't hurt my bare legs when I went down. It was the best time to be at the park, but we couldn't stay. It wasn't a good time to be away from home. Dinner couldn't be late and the noise of cooking bothered my Daddy. It made him mad.

We hurried to the car, Mama had my hand and she was almost running. "Hurry Baby, come on, we've got to get home. I didn't realize how late it was."

I didn't argue with her. I wanted to get there just as fast as she did. I knew what happened if we didn't. Cars got in our way though, stopped at lights, or took a long time to turn. The mailman kept putting mail in people's boxes and Mama banged her hand on the steering wheel.

"Dammit," she said.

His truck wasn't home when we got there and Mama let out a long breath. "Let's hurry," she said.

She had some pork chops in the skillet on the stove and was washing lettuce in the sink when the screen door squeaked. Our heads turned with the slide of the key in the lock. It happened every time the key slid in, even if Mama was humming a song or washing a dish in the sink, she stopped, turned, and watched the doorknob. The key made a scratching sound, then a click and the knob turned.

When he came in the house singing or whistling or carrying a grocery bag, everything would be OK. He might pick me up and swing me around, calling me his doll baby, or kiss Mama and dance her around the kitchen. It didn't happen often, but when it did, we had fun. Even Mama looked happy.

When he came in quiet though, I held my breath. Tonight, he was quiet. The door of the trailer opened into the living room. The sofa faced the kitchen and the tv was between the two. I was sitting on the floor watching my Mama around the noise of the tv.

"Shut that damn racket off," he said.

I turned the knob on the set and backed myself up until I was sitting in the hole between the sofa and the green chair. There was a space just big enough for me to curl into if I pulled my knees up real tight and held them with my arms. I rested my chin on my knees, squeezed my eyes shut and waited.

150

"Where've you been all day?" he asked Mama.

"Here mostly," she said. "It was sunny, so I took Maggie to the park this afternoon for a little while."

"Uh Huh, sure you did," he said, like she was lying. I told the truth too, but he didn't ever seem to believe me either.

He opened the refrigerator to get a beer. I couldn't see, but I could hear the door open and the bottles rattle. The top popped off and rolled around on the kitchen floor. He kicked it and it hit the wall under the window.

"Must have had fun today," he said, "going to the park and all. That why you're all dressed up? That why you have on lipstick?" he asked Mama.

"I'm not all dressed up Mike," she said in a quiet voice with a shake to it.

She wasn't dressed up. She had on a dress, but it was an old one with a hole at the bottom where she got it caught on a nail outside one day. She always wore lipstick.

"Can't I even give my wife a compliment?" he said. "Can't I even tell you you look nice without you arguing?" he said. Then he slammed down the bottle on the table and his voice got louder.

151

"I'm sorry honey," Mama said. She said she was sorry a lot. Most of what she said wasn't right or didn't come out like she meant it to.

"You're sorry alright," he said. "I should have listened to my Mama. She said you were no good. She said you'd run around on me and lie. Too pretty for her own good, she said. Don't go and marry her, you'll regret it, she said."

Mama turned with the lettuce in her hand just in time to catch the back of his hand with her cheek. She spun around in the floor, letting go of the lettuce. It smashed into the kitchen window and bounced off the table onto the floor. Mama fell to a heap at my Daddy's feet. She was curled up, holding her face, and crying.

"Don't lie to me again," he said, picking up his beer and slamming out the front door.

I waited a few minutes, until I heard the truck back up and take off again, scattering rocks against the side of the trailer. I crawled out of my hole and over to my Mama. I sat rubbing her back and crying with her.

"I'm so sorry I made us late," I said. "I won't do it again."

Blue

by Adrienne S Moody

I will never know if it was a dream or if it was real. I ran behind him, not able to catch up. I call to him, but he doesn't turn—he doesn't seem to hear.

He's gone now, dead for nearly seven years. The only time I feel his presence is through my dreams. The other night I had a dream that I was going to travel by car through the Rocky Mountains. I'm on the phone with him and I tell him that I am afraid, that I know that part of this passage is very dangerous.

"I know it is Dad, because I've dreamed about it."

"It's okay. That part is fixed now. It's safe," he tells me, reassuringly.

The rest of the day I have a sense of comfort—a feeling of safety.

Just after he died I was in distress. Not only did I grieve his loss, but the man I was living with was becoming aggressive towards me. Dan knew I didn't love him anymore and he knew that I was preparing to leave. I had moved into a separate bedroom and became very quiet when he was around.

He arrived home one day wearing his hair and beard in a way that made him look sinister. Dan told me the barber didn't want to do it, but that Dan himself had insisted.

"It makes you look...cruel."

"I know," he smiled at me.

I hated him so much. I wanted to wrap my hands around that scrawny neck of his and drown him in his bathtub water. Of course I didn't. I wanted to. I was so dependent on him, financially. I was afraid to live on my own. I was an emotional cripple.

"I stand up tall when he arrives home from work," I tell my grief counselor.

"Why do you do that?"

"Because it's a matter of pecking order. If I sit at the table, then he stands behind me. He just stands there until I sweat. He often blows his nose over me. He did that only once and now I stand immediately when he arrives home. I cannot let him ever feel like he's got the upper hand."

"Is that really necessary, Adrienne?"

"Yes, it is. When I confronted him about making an inappropriate joke about women at the dinner table, he asked me to leave the room with him for only a moment. When I did he grabbed me by the shoulders and pushed me up against the wall."

"What did you do?"

"I pushed him off me and shoved him against the wall."

"And?…"

"He told me later on that he would beat me if I wasn't as strong as I was."

"Adrienne, the only thing that disturbs me about all of this…"

"Yes?"

"…is the fact that you've lived with this man so long and never realized his abuse towards you."

"Well, at least I know it now."

"So what will you do?"

"Leave as soon as I'm financially able."

I had weak moments.

I told my son after we spent the day looking for other accommodation, "Maybe Dan will change. Maybe we could give him another chance."

"What makes you think he's going to change, Mom?"

He was right. I tucked my son in that night with my cheeks wet. I was so afraid—afraid of the unknown future, afraid of being alone.

I went to bed in my own room and slept fitfully, dreaming that I heard my Dan calling angrily out to my son. He yelled at him to come to him. I sat up in bed, heart pounding. Was it real? Or a dream? I went to my son's room and he was asleep. It was a dream. I knew the dream was a warning to leave before my son was harmed.

I slept once more, dreaming I was in a school, wandering aimlessly, looking for my locker—I knew I was in the Blue Section—all the lockers were blue, and I find the Blue Section, and begin to look for mine, but a woman looking older, and so wise, and so kind, takes my hand and says, "you don't have to be here anymore, follow me" and I do, like a maze through corridors and doors, and then a big heavy door leads suddenly outside, and it's a neighborhood, with a house built of stone and ivy growing all over, and it looks and feels to me so strong, and so, so, so safe, and she says, with a wave of her hand, you can choose this—and I wake up.

The rain pounded relentlessly on the windshield. Dan and I sat in silence, waiting in the car—I was in the driver's seat. I still drove him to the bus waiting for #351 to take him to the city to his office.

"Swisha, swisha" the windshield wipers clear and then blur, clear and blur. Silence.

"I had a strange dream last night," he spoke finally.

I can't look at him. I hate him so very much.

"Hmmm."

"I had a dream that my hands were full of these sucker like... things... and I would latch onto anything blue... and snuff the life out..."

"Swisha, swisha, swisha."   Blur, clear. Blur, clear.

"That's really bizarre, Dan."

"Bizarre?"

"There's your bus..."

I sat there after his bus pulled away and disappeared. I knew my dad was there, but I didn't know how long he could continue to help me. I knew the two dreams were what I needed in order to face my uncertain future.

I went home and packed our belongings. Thanks Dad.

Family Picnics

by M Dawn Thacker

Grandpa gathered his family. He did it by way of his voice, and food. "We'll plan a picnic," he'd say, and all would ask when and where? When I was a little girl, picnics were at his house, the small white cinderblock structure on 250 West near Crozet. He owned two acres of land, which seemed to us children to stretch forever, from sky to ground and from the highway to the river. We collected flowers in spring, berries in summer, red and orange leaves in the fall, and cold toes in the winter. Picnics from November through March were held indoors, but dishes were laid out on the red checked tablecloth nonetheless. We gathered at Grandpa's feet and listened to his stories.

My cousin Judy recently completed chemo treatments for breast cancer. She's been battling the sickness and fatigue. We cousins are more like siblings. We call to check on each other and share news, even if it's about what bug is chewing on our tomato vines. We've all worried about Judy and take turns calling her so we don't overwhelm. The telephone tree works like our family tree, with deep roots and far reaching branches. We get the news one way or another.

We were all relieved when Judy called a family picnic. It would be held at her house on June 6th. It was good news, she was feeling better. Everybody got busy. My Mama made potato salad from Grandma's recipe, coleslaw, deviled eggs, two custard pies, two damson caramel pies, and an apple brandy cake. The rest of us brought one dish or dessert apiece. The menu ended up being fried chicken, macaroni and cheese, Aunt Connie's squash casserole, broccoli casserole, baked beans and a carved watermelon basket filled with fresh cherries, blueberries, grapes and of course, watermelon. Desserts, other than Mama's, were rum cake, cherry cobbler, double chocolate brownies (Scott's world famous), and carrot cake with cream cheese frosting. There was enough food to feed all of us, the neighbors, their relatives and even Grandpa had he been there. Mama gave the blessing and thanked everyone, including God, for Judy's strength and recovery.

Picnics mean eating, storytelling, sitting on porch swings, and laughing so hard our stomachs hurt. We take turns, repeating and reliving those earlier years in our lives when Grandpa, Grandma, Aunts, Uncles and all the cousins were together.

Mama told us about sleigh riding with her beagles, Jack and Jerry, when she was a little girl. She'd stay out in the snow until she turned blue or Grandma made her come in. The dogs took turns riding down the hill with her on the sled, their droopy ears flapping in the wind.

Rebecca told us about visiting Mama and Daddy when they lived in Hampton, how she came to the beach and had all visions of lying in the sun, catching a boyfriend, and relaxing on her summer vacation. Instead, she babysat me, helped with dishes and got homesick.

Emily talked about the time she and I rode the Amtrak train to Washington DC when Uncle Garnett was the conductor, how we thought we were so grown up, traveling in our fancy dresses and hats. We were ten and seven. Emily has gray hair now and looks an awful lot like her Mama.

Judy told the story about the time she recorded Grandpa for a school project. He didn't like the microphone, said it made him feel like he was supposed to be more than what he was. They discussed his relatives back as far as he could remember his great-grandfather, Daniel, grandfather, Jim, and his father Henry Mortimer. Judy learned that Grandpa's own Daddy was "Not much count for anything. He was educated like I wish I had been," Grandpa said, "But he didn't care a lick about his family." Grandpa loved and respected his mother though. "I promised to take care of her until the day she died, and I did," he said.

They took a walk in the garden, pulled some potatoes up to see how they were coming along, and discussed the feud between the Hatfields and McCoys. A program had aired on television the night before. "Don't ever have a falling out over something as minor as a pig, like them people did," Grandpa had told Judy. "People will hold a grudge and not speak to each other until it's too late to make amends. It's hard to tell a dead person you love 'em," he said.

At the end of the day, we gathered in Judy's driveway to hug each other goodbye. She had a surprise for each of us. She had made a CD of her interview with Grandpa and presented one to each of us.

I didn't put the CD into the player until I was alone in the car this morning on my way to work. I pulled out of the driveway leading from his house, my house now, and turned onto Rt. 250 toward town. Thirty years melted away as I listened to his voice, telling his stories. The interview was on a family picnic day. Grandpa was watching for members of the family and he would announce each one's arrival right in the middle of a story. "There's Carolyn," he said while talking about his raspberries. "Here comes Iris," I heard him a bit later, interrupting his musings about Snoopy, the neighbor's dog. Shortly after each exclamation of arrival the machine would switch off and I'm sure

162

it was so he could give a hug and a kiss. When it turned back on he'd answer another question and a new story would begin. The last thing he said before the interview ended was, "I'm getting kind of hungry, but when have you known me not to be?" And he laughed, just like I remembered.

On the Fridge Door
by Adrienne S Moody

How they change over the years, or do they? I am referring to the odd bits and pieces that we pin to the fridge door with magnets. I thought of this today as I've recently moved and have only a few last things to unpack. Pressed between pages of the phone book are my fridge treasures. I scanned them all and am not ready to part with any of them:

-The card from a flower shop where I bought two roses to put on my parents' grave. It reads simply, *"I Love You."* I only visited the grave site once. It was a bitter cold winter day and because of the plaques only policy, I had a very difficult time trying to find their burial site. But I did. I remember my footsteps crunching on the icy snow. I placed the blood red roses on the white ground where I knew their bodies lay below.

-A small whiteboard with my son's address and postal code of the apartment he and his new bride were moving into. At the bottom he wrote: *I love you, mom. Hope you have a good nite. Love, Steve.* I remember the sound of the screen door slamming when he left with the last of his belongings. I remember the quiet after the sound of his car faded and he was gone.

-A newspaper article kept for inspiration. The headline reads: 'Two B.C. novelists among finalists for $25,000 Writers' Trust Prize'

-A picture of the family home I grew up in. My neighbor visited my town and asked for my old address. She offered to take a picture of my childhood home. I said, "Why not?" Now I have it. Many of my stories are written about the goings on there and the street we lived on. How small it is. To think eight people lived there is beyond comprehension.

-A picture painted by some artist on a card that absolutely captures the atmosphere of the prairies. There is a crumbling fence post and behind, a golden wheat field. The sky is dark purple. I remember the smell of rain approaching and the electricity in the air just before an electric storm would make the hair on my arms stand on end.

-And my favorite: an old black and white photo of my mom kneeling down next to me. I am maybe 2 years old and her head is pressed to mine. She is wearing an old fashioned print dress and her hair looks full with curls and I know is auburn in color. I am wearing a baby's dress with a flared skirt and I'm pointing to the camera, probably at my father. There is a shadow of a tree stretched out in front of us. Now that image reminds me of the shadow that continually haunted the relationship between her and I.

-A long narrow black fridge magnet with the words: ***Do not limit the future by the past.***

-And the Secret Credo: The first two lines: ***I Promise Myself. To be so strong that nothing can disturb my peace of mind.***

Old Coat

by Gaboo

I found an old coat and memory flooded back. There were bits of paper in the pocket and it still carried the scent of stale tobacco and too many hours in the pub. The weave was as coarse as I remembered, but the liner was still smooth. In a moment I drifted back to a toddler's day in the cold prairie winter, bundled in the warmth of the old coat, confident in the security of the wearer. It was the familiar shell of man with a worried collar and stained elbows. A working man's coat. A tired uniform without distinction. Any man's coat. A father's coat. And when I tried it on, memory evaporated and the sentiment fled. It was my coat.

The Visit

by M Dawn Thacker

An orange tiger-striped kitten is no substitute for a father, even if the cat is male, and comes to live full time in a little girl's house. A mother should know that.

My father was leaving again. My fingers tightened into the back of his shirt, my arms and legs were like little skinny bands tied tightly to his upper body. He was trying to finish hugging me goodbye. I was trying to hold onto the last little bit of love I could manage. I couldn't see when I lifted my head because the water was too thick, and I couldn't explain what I needed because my voice wouldn't work right. My throat was too tight. He was trying to push me away and my mother was trying to pull me off him. Both of them were talking to me, wanting me to stop crying and clinging, wanting me to give up the struggle so that everything could return to normal. My father needed to rush off to some other part of the world and my mother needed to pull me inside the apartment and close the door, so things could go back to the way they were before. My sound was a wail; my grief was determined.

He showed up every six months, fresh off the ocean, tall, handsome, and bearing gifts from foreign lands: a set of dolls with costumes and matching hats; a tiny leather purse with stitched labels of "Paris", "London", "Madrid", and "Toyko"; a royal blue tapestry decorated with solid white kittens; and two days of his time.

My mother's demeanor changed each time my father called. Her smile faded, her head dropped into her hand and she rubbed at her temples with her thumb and middle fingers. She spoke with a simple "yes" or "no." I sensed her despair and my excitement grew. My Daddy was home and was coming for me.

We had fun, went to the park, rode the little train through the tunnel. He folded up his long legs so he could sit beside me, his strong arm wrapped around my shoulder, his sunglasses on my face. He smelled like spice and his face was a little scratchy. We laughed and ate ice cream and drove fast with the top of the car folded down behind the back seat. My hair blew into my eyes, and it didn't matter.

While he was in town, we stayed at my Grandma's house. Her kitchen smelled like black pepper. We sat at her red, Formica and chrome table, eating pot roast that was 'pull-apart' tender, green beans cooked with new potatoes on top, corn pudding baked golden with yellow kernels nestled in custard. Grandma's biscuits rose thick and hot. Her homemade blackberry jam dripped out the sides, all the food, my Daddy's favorites. He told adventure stories at the supper table. The Navy sounded exciting with sunny ports and big adventures. My Grandma looked at him like I wished my Mama would.

Two days went as fast as six months went slow. Before my father left, I watched the clock over the mantle in my Grandma's living room. The second hand ticked his time away, pushing me closer and closer to my mother, further and further away from him. I couldn't talk in the car. I was too busy holding back tears that were trying to rush out.

"No tears," my Daddy said, "we've had too much fun to cry."

I couldn't stop crying. It was like I had saved up gallons of tears and when I couldn't hold them in anymore, couldn't be brave, couldn't do the one thing he asked me to do—I had already failed—why try? He was gone.

Every six months, he turned his back and left me crying. My mother, feeling helpless, was left to try to put a small broken child back together.

"I found something special for you," Mama said, her hands behind her back.

169

I looked up, tears running off my chin. I still couldn't talk, but my mother had a gesture. She smiled at me and presented me with a small, orange-striped kitten. I reached out and took the ball of soft fur and held him in my arms as I cried, my tears making wet spots on his fur. He was nice, but he wasn't my Daddy.

Father, Where Are You
by Sarah Scott

strong weathered hand, rough against mine
side by side in the grocery line
my short stature, his lanky frame
our one thing in common is our last name
his eyes are brown, mine are blue
his skin is leather, mine smooth
brown hair turned gray, once resembled mine
but changes and fades with the passing of time
a moment of pure love, creation of life
with a little girl born in the pale moonlight
cradled in his arms—rocked to sleep in his chair—
oh what I would give to be with him there
before life changed him, before the booze won
when I meant his all, and all else meant none
his strong weathered hand, rough against mine
side by side in a grocery line

Read This Please

Volume 1 Edition 4 - Harvest Edition

September 22, 2010

It's wonderful of you to stop by at this time. The autumnal equinox occurs right about now, as the Sun appears to move over the celestial equator traveling north to south. Thus begins the Harvest. Let us take stock of a summer in thoughts and experiences, and celebrate what we've gathered.

First Taste of Fall
by M Dawn Thacker

Today was cooler than it has been all week. The humidity was low and we had highs in the seventies. A breeze blew all day long and clothes dried quickly on the line. The sky held the color of my grandma's blue willow china. There were a few white clouds that drifted in and out. The heat of last week was gone and autumn felt closer.

I wanted apples, not the ones from the grocery store, but the ones from the orchard. Miller School owns an apple orchard not far from our house. The boys who attended Miller used to do the picking and packing in return for part of their tuition payment, but since the school has become more of a college preparatory institution, with parents willing and able to shell out the money, boys no longer do the work, migrant farm workers from Mexico do.

We know the back roads to the orchard and plan our visits after the picking has been done. We cull the leftovers and usually bring home a grocery bag of whatever is ripe. Today, we collected golden delicious. The apples that are left are usually in

173

the tops of the trees or hanging on branches that have been broken off by machinery. We couldn't resist the temptation and found ourselves biting into one before washing it. Rubbing it briskly on our shirt was good enough cleaning. There's nothing like the taste of the first bite of ripe apple off the tree. The crunch, and juice running off your chin, makes you close your eyes and remember. That apple tastes just like autumn.

Pacifica

by Steven Bird

Behind the mountains. A thin moon casts shadows down the cypress and oak and over the long pastures spread to bluffs receiving the sea. Dana hopes he doesn't hit a deer, rolls the window down. The interior floods with the scents of cypress, sage, fish and cow dung. It brings him more awake. He sips his coffee and glances west seeing only a pane of black. The odd wink of moonlit foam.

Dana unlocks the back door to the San Simeon Sport Fishing operation, turns the lights on in the shop, then rolls out the little orchard tractor used to haul the fishing gear out to the end of the pier for loading on the boats. A south swell today. Weird day. Things are switching around. Dana observes. He watches a boat leave the cove, round the point and head into the swell. The sea and early sky are the same color gray.

David Dean D.D.S. fastens his wetsuit between the vehicles parked in the driveway. Dave and Tiffany drive the Navigator and two B'mers. He takes up his board and jogs down to the beach. The gunmetal swells are growing. He paddles out and sits his

175

board on the glassy calm. The ocean rises and falls. Dave waits, letting a few sets slip through while he gets the rhythm. The fourth wave in the set will be the best. The ocean expands. Rises. He strokes into it. Drops over the edge. A brown pelican folds its wings, plunges like a collapsed umbrella into the backside. Dave thinks it's the best ride he's had in a month, wishes he had more time to surf. He regrets some of the choices he's made. Tiffany is not awake yet, seldom goes to the beach, doesn't like the wind.

A faded blue '72 Ford step-van squats at the edge of a wide gravel shoulder along the road above the lighthouse. Close to Arroyo de la Cruz. Pipe Man steps out, sets a pot of coffee on a butane burner set up on the ground. He opens the back door to the rig exposing the interior lined with colorful tapestries. He unfolds a small folding table and arranges the pipes in a pleasing order on the table top. The pipes are beautifully carved from stones gathered at Jade Cove. Pipe Man hopes somebody will stop and try one.

A compact brown man wearing baggy shorts, Hawaiian shirt and a broad-brimmed hat emerges from under the Pico Creek bridge carrying a driftwood walking stick and a green day pack. He hikes to the San Simeon store where he takes a seat on a bench under a bay laurel tree. His pack contains bits of abalone shell strung on small circles of bead chain. He hopes to sell enough of the key chains to buy a quart of beer. His children in Wisconsin have given up the search for him.

The brightening cove, sliver of beach, the cypress windbreak on the point, remind Dana of an oriental painting, crescent moon fading in the daylight background. Crab-walking, pipe-smoking, black-heart Capt. Chuck is giving Dana the rundown on the jobs he wants done. They notice a small salmon trawler coming toward the pier. Fuckin Moriarty, Chuck rasps, they know they're not supposed to use the ramp. A pretty young woman with long brown hair appears, hustles past dragging a brown sea-bag, hurrying down the pier to meet the boat. Get on the Deere, run out there and stop them. They can use the ladder at the end of the pier. Insurance don't cover them using our ramp. Chuck knows the old iron ladder isn't safe, fastenings rusted through, and difficult to approach in a south swell.

The Moriarty is maneuvering toward the restricted ramp. The girl waits on the platform. Dana knows it's the safest place for her to board. He doesn't want to stop them. He envies the young skipper with the sunbleached hair operating the immaculate troller. HEY! he hollers to the skipper. They don't want you using the ramp...

The girl is doe-eyed, tragic. The skipper yells back: Are you a moron? I'm pickin her up, here, and I don't care what you say.

Dana doesn't say anything. The girl hands the bag across, then springs aboard the boat.

Capt. Chuck, blood veins standing out on his neck, spit droplets fleeing from his mouth, rages at Dana for failing the mission. Dana tells him to stick the job up his ass. The cove at San Simeon is the first place the sun breaks through the coastal gray. The sky is an iridescent pearl, blue, pink, abalone shell.

David Dean takes his after-surf shower. He plans to drive Tiffany up to Big Sur today. She's upstairs in the kitchen having her coffee with French Vanilla creamer. She won't drink it any other way. Her hair is smartly clipped in a pageboy, parted on the side, the ends brushing her neck. She is Texas born and raised. Dallas. Her daddy is a minor wheel at a plastic injection molding company and, after some convincing arguments from the mother, paid for the topside work that caught Dave's attention, initially. They met at a Methodist college. Within a week of meeting Dave, Tiffany changed her course of study from interior design to dentistry so they could have classes together. She tried going into practice with him after they graduated, but she proved inept. She decided that she hated putting her fingers into people's mouths. She's been feeling depressed lately. She is certain that it is because of the sinks. The sinks not being right. Marble sinks. That's what she needs. She knows if she had marble sinks the

178

depression would go away and her life could get on track again. She wants Dave to take on more patients, not surf so much.

Beyond the eucalyptus, where the surfers park, a thin stream course leads to the tilted rocks of Hazard Reef. A diminutive freshwater trace is all that is left of an ancient river that flowed broad and powerful to the sea, depositing a deep golden delta. The little stream pours into a tide pool holding flat, gray and yellow stones, like coinage, with perfect holes through them. If you have a question, want to know the way of things, you can look through the hole in one of these stones and see the answer, see how things really are. Freddy rinses his surf booties in the tide pool while the humping swells crest and rush over the reef. The booming assault echoes from the yellow cliffs. He is worried, praying that his wife will beat the cancer. He's dyed his hair blue, to match the sea and sky. He doesn't know about the stones.

The Cambria girl arrives at the cove. She spreads her blanket up the beach and slips off her India print skirt and top, shakes out her thick black hair. She is beautiful. Chestnut-brown and full. The dark triangle between her legs is thick, untrimmed. She crosses the beach to the water, wades out, dives through the face of a breaking wave and swims like a brown seal. She emerges dripping and cold and walks back to lie on her blanket. When the sun warms her loins enough, she receives a curious notion. The

179

thought flares, she entertains it for a moment, chases it away. The breeze rises, courses to whip the waves lashing the wild shore, buffets the affluent lines of traffic flowing up and down the bright highway.

At Montana de Oro three boys hike a trail winding through sage and scrub oak, leading them along the edge of a cliff rising a hundred feet above the beach, the trail breaks away from the cliff, the portion of ground dissolves mid-air from under their feet, the illusion of solidity dissipating as they fall. Two boys land on soft sand. One boy lands against rock. Later, his mother will promise a ponderous atonement.

Smokey one-way glass windows hide the interior of a tour bus idling in the Ragged Point parking lot while its cargo of tiny Asian visitors cluster on the cliff edge like penguins on an ice chunk. One old woman remains on the bus, refusing to come outside. She is terrified of the steepness.

Dave would rather they'd driven one of the BMW's. Tiffany doesn't like the seats in the Navigator but knows that the road to Big Sur often falls from the sides of the mountains into the sea. She thinks the four-wheel-drive might come in handy if it happens. Dave reflects on the life insurance policies they've recently purchased.

Two hours past high tide, old Henry climbs the bluff above Moonstone. Reaching the top he stands to catch his breath. A carved heron watching the cars flash by on the highway. He carries an eleven-foot Harnell surf rod. On his back rests a black rubber pack containing about seven pounds of barred perch and a few thin calico surfperch – the whole thing worth about ten dollars to the fish buyer in Morro Bay. Heavy loads of perch on better days, and a hip replacement, have diminished his stature, but he is remarkably healthy for eighty-five. Nobody going by in the cars knows anything about the perch business and none will choose it as a career. He thinks, tomorrow, he'll try above the lighthouse. Plastic Beach, maybe.

Nuances of wind, tide and geology converge at Plastic to produce a gyre in local ocean currents. The prevailing Oregon Current sweeping down the coast is loaded with debris carried down by river and flood. Branches, logs, stumps, the timbers of old homestead barns. And with this comes a considerable amount of man-made items, particularly plastic. Chairs with legs missing, garbage containers split from rim to bottom, fuel containers, milk-jugs, juice-jugs, bait-jugs, soda bottles, water bottles, parts of dolls, torn tarpaulins, sheets of clear plastic, medication bottles, hospital bracelets, the occasional syringe, Big Gulp cups, lids, straws – the plastic gathers in the eddy and washes ashore on Plastic Beach. You park at the turnout, get through the barbed-

181

wire fence, then cross the Hearst bull pasture to the bluff
overlooking the beach. From the bluff you are delighted to see
what looks like a parti-colored crowd of Saturday beach goers
thronging the warm crescent – umbrellas pitched, blankets,
towels, jugs, beach balls and frisbees laid out. But when you get
down the bluff to the beach, you find a forlorn, windblown,
wrecked-circus landscape where the multi-colored indelible
plastic quivers against tangled driftwood laced with drying,
sandblasted kelp. The beach balls are flattened. Frisbees broken.
There isn't a soul. Sea.

Sunlight floods through gum and cypress branches to splash
against the Sebastian store's peeling false-front. A string of
Tibetan bells nailed to the door tinkle as Dana swings inward.
He's back for more beer. The pretty, middle-aged woman
stationed by the ornate antique cash resister smiles him a
welcome. He stumbles across the splintered plank floor to the
cold case. The door clinks again and Tiffany Dean bustles in,
marches straight to the case, selects two bottles of flavored water,
brushes against Dana's arm on her way to the cash register, pays
for the water, and the door tinkles shut again. Dana grabs a plastic
wrapped sandwich and a six-pack of beer. He won't eat the
sandwich and doesn't need the beer. The stuff in the case blurs.
The store tilts. He's having a hard time walking on that damned
slanting floor. With studied determination he makes it to the cash

register and drops the things down on the counter. The woman, bra-less under a red t-shirt, smiles. But the smile doesn't seem right. Doesn't work. Nothing seems right. And nothing works. He thinks the reception is off, reaches across the counter…

A tattooed man shouldering a heavy pack trudges north toward the Big Sur highlands. A turkey vulture rides a thermal, rising, circling, head tilting, eyes sharp for road kill. The pack contains everything the man owns. Among his things there is a worn copy of *The Seven Pillars of Zen*. Dave and Tiffany pass without seeing him. He doesn't turn his head.

Silver wave tops disintegrate in the afternoon wind. The lonesome bluffs, the open sensuous roll of foothill pastures, combine to produce an undefined sweet longing, a strange melancholy that does not lie heavy but somehow lightens the heart. There is a vague promise at the ragged western edge of the continent, compelling the traveler to question boundaries, and drop inhibitions. I can never really connect to it, Tiffany emotes. Dave doesn't answer. Silence pulses in the air-conditioned SUV. It is a lost coast, isn't it, she whispers to herself. She starts to think about the marble sinks again. Pipe Man stands up from his table as they pass him going north.

Tiffany rinses her mouth with mandarin flavored water. The steering wheel is sticky from Dave's palms. They round a bend and he turns the Navigator on to a dirt turnout above a high promontory, not far from Pacific Valley. He and Tiffany get out and walk to the edge of a three hundred-foot drop to the rocks. They stand at the brink. The ocean spreads out like milk. Rough mountains jut from the trailing rim behind them, dangerous, angular, inhumanely steep. They watch the ocean redden as the sun descends to the horizon line. Dave's fingers slide against Tiffany's shoulder, hesitant. His palms are wet, at the end of everything. He glances toward the highway, then to the rocks. White confetti gulls wheel below their feet. Inertia draws them toward the void. A salt breeze surges against their faces. His arm tightens. The moment burns, where the road breaks and slides from the mountains. Tiffany says, "I'm scared, we're too close to the edge."

"Yes, we are", Dave answers.

He pulls her back a comfortable distance. They watch the atmosphere bend and distort the light coming into the world, the red sun flattening against the tao sea, where waves of the ocean dance and dance.

The Planets Are Lining Up

by Adrienne S Moody

(Mature: some coarse language)

Elaine called twice and I've not called her back, so today I picked up the phone and dialed her number. I'm feeling hopeful and happy; the sun is shining and my son is doing better. I have that dangerous feeling that I'm somehow in control of my life, so I can afford to risk a call to her.

"Everything is going well," I told her.

"Steve?"

"Yeah, his dad said he's quit smoking pot, so I'm going to believe him and I believe he's going to be okay. And M and I are still plugging along. I hate feeling dependent, Elaine. When I feel dependent on a guy. I start having these expectations and then I'm just inviting disappointment. I think I should just have him as a lover and forget living together. Maybe that is the answer. How are you?"

"Well, Rob's picking up the baby on Friday."

"Good."

"Yes, he's flying there and coming straight back. And I'm a little...scared actually."

"Why?"

"Well, there goes our freedom. I'm going to be a mom again. That's scary to me."

"Yeah."

"I have to prepare this statement to read in court to a judge which has to explain why Mark and his girlfriend are unfit to parent..." Her voice quivered and I heard her sobbing away from the phone. I waited. "It's so hard to read the words on paper that my son is such a fuck-up."

"It would be hard to read those words."

"It is. It's one thing to know it and talk to family about it. But, it's another thing talking to authority and admitting this to them."

"It makes it more real, maybe? But, maybe it's good that this is a process you're going through, Elaine. A higher level of acceptance, because you can't control their behavior."

"No, I know. So yeah, maybe it is. They're never going to quit. They can't and never will."

"I don't believe that. I've quit my addictions and it wasn't easy. But, you have to be so....determined. You have to work at skills to help you through those tough times that everyone has. The planets lined up for me one day and I just did it. I reached my bottom. And although my addictions were not as deadly as your kids, they were still addictions. I feel empathy for anyone addicted to anything. I think these drugs that are out there do so much damage to the mind that there isn't anything left to work with."

"I think you're right."

"Wish I wasn't. I gotta go. Please don't ever think I don't want to talk to you. If I don't call back, call again. Okay?"

"I don't want to bring you down. You're happy. I don't want all this crap to bring you down."

"It doesn't," I lied.

We hung up and I loaded up my car with everything a girl needs to be away for a couple of days. Everything from hiking boots to curling iron and everything in between. I stopped at my thrift for the third time today and scored five rose-colored hand towels for a buck each. I said goodbye to the girls I know by name and stopped here at the Small Ritual Cafe for a cup of tea and a write.

Life is good. For now.

Grain Elevators
by Sheila Cano

Bordered on one side by the inlet, on the other by the train tracks, the grain elevators are both ugly and beautiful as industrial architecture. Looming how many stories high? Six? Eight? Tall cylindrical silos stand joined by the length of a building with massive curling ducts spilling down the sides like giant intestines—an almost Gothic appearance, a brooding atmosphere. At night, different coloured lights illuminate the expanse of concrete and steel, glowing sodium orange or eerie green. Ladders become spidery silhouettes against the exterior.

I became fascinated with the building, driving home at night. The railway runs beside the road and the rounded grain cars form a diagonal curve along the tracks, like a snake receding into the distance. Red and green lights punctuate empty space at intervals above the tracks. Oncoming auto headlights glare in yellowish, white, or piercing halogen blue-pink floating past red and orange taillights of the vehicles ahead of me. In the thirty seconds or so that it takes to drive past this scene, I become filled with awe— here is a monstrosity of human activity. The site hums day and night with the urgency of commerce, the enormity of an

188

agricultural commodity finding its way from bulging grain cars to the bowels of a building, and onto the great holds of ships that pause alongside in the salt chuck.

The urge to photograph or paint the site has gnawed at me for years. The proximity of the railway, the road, and the steep hillside leaves little room to safely stop and record the scene. There is a cycle path running parallel to the road for a short distance; that might be a vantage point, but I would have to walk from a busy three-way intersection near a lumber yard. I am intimidated by the logistics of finding a place to stop, draw a picture, and not get run over.

Apple Butter
by M Dawn Thacker

It happens every year, and still, it sneaks up on me. Each September I watch my husband prepare, so it shouldn't surprise me, but it always does. I go out to the porch to water my geraniums and hear the crack and splinter of wood under axe. The air is still and hot, not very conducive to splitting wood. My awareness shifts, and I know he's down behind the garage, sweating and stretching his muscles, dividing lengths of branch and limb into halves and quarters. The pieces are piling up into a small mountain beside him. That's when I remember. It's almost apple butter time. I love the spicy thickness of it when spooned onto a hot buttered biscuit, but I dread making it. It's my husband's family tradition, not mine, and it's hard work.

In another week or so, I'll overhear the telephone conversation Bruce has with his eighty-three year old father. "I'm thinking the week of October twenty-third. You got plans that weekend?—OK, put it down and we'll shoot for that—No I got plenty wood. You just make sure the stand is in good shape and get the kettle out and clean it up. We don't have to patch any holes in it do we?—Alright, We'll call Ben and see if he can come home from school that weekend. We need all the help we can get."

Next, I'll hear him scratching around in the attic, banging his head and cursing. He'll call me to the stairs that fold out of the ceiling and he'll be bent over up there, feeding the long-handled wooden stirring paddle down the steps to me. Next will come the glass canning jars and rings stored in wooden apple boxes. I'll stack them in the hallway. The upstairs is unbearable this time of year. There's little ventilation, and the air is thick, but the temperature doesn't seem to bother Bruce when he's on a mission. He drips sweat, but smiles.

He's already scoped out the apple orchards, anticipating the exact moment of perfect ripeness. He has marked his internal calendar with the date for harvesting. The weather should be cooler then, and with four of us working, gathering fifteen to twenty bushels of Stamen or Winesap apples will only take most of an afternoon. Of course, we'll have to clean out the bed of the pick up truck before we leave so the wooden apple crates will slide in side by side until there's no more room. After the bed is full, we stack them. Four of us no longer fit in the cab of the truck, so we'll have to leave room for Ryan on the back. He's the smallest.

Picking the apples is the fun part. I can sneak away, pull out my camera, take photos of the knotty trees, their branches hanging low with rust-colored fruit. I catch Ryan in the act of throwing an apple at his brother's back and Ben's scowl when he turns. Bruce laughs, half an apple in his hand, juice running off his chin. He wipes it with the sleeve of his shirt. He admonishes, "Get back to work. We'll never get finished at this rate."

In the week prior to the big day, peeling coring and slicing ensues. The basement of my in-law's house boasts an assembly line of apple preparation. Wooden orchard crates filled with a combination of winesaps and stamen line the floor. Hand crank peelers and corers are clamped to tables. I can close my eyes and hear the sounds, the snap of apple skin breaking, the whir of the blade spiraling through the apple as juice runs, the plunk of cores landing in five gallon plastic buckets, the murmur of voices remembering generations of tradition passed down.

"My Mama used this same knife. It has a nice curve to the blade, perfect for the shape of an apple. Her hands were small, like mine."

"Your Granddaddy took the peelings and a little bit of cider vinegar and scrubbed the inside of the apple butter kettle with them every year. He worked that mixture around until the inside of the kettle shined like a new penny."

"We weren't choosy about what kind of apples we used way back then. We used what we could find and pick up under the trees. No difference in taste as far as I can see. That mix years ago might have even been a bit better than what we make today."

"My hand is tired, can I go watch tv now?"

"Of course you can, this work is hard on a little fella."

I want to join the little fella, my back and shoulders are tired, the apple skins have stained my hands and I'm sticky from my fingers to my elbows. There are ten full boxes left. What are we going to do with all this apple butter? I'm content with one or two jars a season. Not Bruce, he's content with no less than a farm table full of quart and pint jars.

My mother-in-law forgoes the fancy machines for a sharp paring knife. She has a rhythm to her peeling and the wooden handle of the knife feels familiar to her hand. Her peelings are skin thin and spiral into the bucket in one long piece. These along with the cores, stems and seeds are treats for the cows.

Apples are sliced thin and the raw pieces are put in plastic bags in a cool corner of the room. The night before we make the apple butter, they'll be washed. We will cook on Saturday. By Friday night there are six or seven, thirty-gallon plastic bags of apples, waiting.

Apple butter making starts early. The fire is built under the pot at four o'clock in the morning. It's dark and cold when we slip from between warm bed covers, put on clothes in layers and drive the three miles to my in-law's farm. The firewood is stacked on the trailer behind our pickup. The jars and metal rings, clean and shiny, are packed in boxes. New rubber-ringed lids are the only things we haven't recycled. They are new. A wash tub holds five pound sacks of sugar, tiny bottles of cinnamon and clove oil, a jug of apple cider, canning funnels, long-handled wooden spoons, metal dippers and some clean dish towels. Ryan, who's been excited all week about the event, grumbles and mumbles as he drags himself out of the truck and into one of Grandma's extra beds until after sunrise.

The men heft the forty-gallon copper apple butter kettle into the cast iron stand, pour in the jug of cider, add one plastic bag of apples and build a fire under the kettle. The apples must be stirred non-stop from beginning to end, otherwise they stick to the kettle and burn.

The wooden stir paddle is old, fashioned by hand out of pine with wooden pegs holding it together. It's been passed down through generations, repaired as necessary, and stored across the rafters in the attic for safe keeping between apple butter makings. The handle is eight feet long, the paddle attached to its end at a

194

ninety degree angle is two feet long, one inch thick. It is a flat, bowling pin shaped piece of wood with holes drilled through to allow the apple butter passage. The corners at the bottom of the paddle are rounded to conform to the sides of the kettle. Stirring "twice around the outside and through the middle once" keeps the apple butter from sticking. Some people drop three or four pennies into the pot. Tradition says it keeps the butter from sticking, or brings good luck.

Bruce's Daddy doesn't believe in using pennies. "It scratches the copper finish on the pot," he says. "Besides, pennies are dirty."

People come and go all day long, relatives, neighbors, and some townsfolk who've gotten wind of the event. Even a few dogs drop by to see what's going on. They are apt to lie in a spot of sun, dozing. Some of the older men do the same thing. Visitors take turns stirring, along with members of the family, while others sit around on apple boxes or stumps and tell stories. Everyone has a different recipe or way of making apple butter. Each family adheres to its own set of rules and ingredients.

The women spend the day keeping the stirrers fed. No one comes in to eat at the kitchen table. Food is set up outdoors, drinks and sweet tea are kept cold in coolers. If the men really wanted to help prepare the food they could. There's no rule, it's just that men tend to stay as far away from the house and as close to the kettle as they can. Men say they don't gossip, but tractors, farmland and machinery carry secrets. Women know.

Bruce's Daddy makes the decisions about when to add more apples as the others "cook down", when to season the apple butter, and when it's thick enough to pull the fire out. It has to pass the spoon and plate test. If it doesn't run when you tilt the plate or spoon, it's ready. Somewhere close to five o'clock in the evening, the apple butter is thick and dark enough to put in jars.

It is ladled into large pots at the kettle and brought to the basement for jarring. The lids are already immersed in boiling water and the jars have been "hotted." Bruce's Mama pours boiling water from the kettle over them. The water is emptied from the jars and apple butter is funneled into them. A lid is removed from the pot of boiling water, placed on top of the jar, and the ring is screwed on tight. The full Mason jar gets a swift wipe with the dishcloth and is set on the farm table to seal. When every bit of the apple butter is jarred there are about twenty gallons (all quart and pint jars). After the clean up, we sit around the wood stove in the basement and listen to the "pop" of the jars as they seal. The jars are divided evenly between the workers. We usually consume two to three quarts during a winter. The other twenty-odd jars are given as gifts.

I walked out onto the porch today, watering can in hand, giving my geraniums a drink. I heard the familiar crack and thunk of wood being split. It's the fifth of September. Apples are hanging on the trees up the road and Bruce is getting ready. Three miles to the east of us, his Daddy is standing in the shed eying the copper kettle. He's expecting a phone call in the next week or so. Tradition demands it.

An Ancient Art
by Sarah Scott

The limbs are naked, withered arms reaching for the gin jar in the high cupboard, leathery skin sagging from the hinges. Feeble and freezing in the first light of morning, he stands stark against the skyline, tired muscles aching, eyes drooping.

The harsh morning chill gives way to afternoon breezes. A little life seeps through weary bones. Green eyes twinkle in sunny glow. Sprigs of hope, ideas and afternoon plans take shape. An hour in the garden. A stroll down the lane. Sitting on the porch sipping tea with a friend.

The fullness of the day, rich warmth brightens his tawny complexion. A toothless grin on his dimpled face. An old-timer sharing stories from youth. A chuckle, a cackle, a knee-slapping roar. He shakes with delight. He bends and sways with grace belying his age.

Evening falls. Golden and crimson streak across the sky. His aged hands still. He stands with radiant, full branches basking in the setting sun.

Running Out of Time
by Thomas Pryce

I just want to run, like I once did when I was a kid, effortlessly and pain-free, fast and easy, like I can still do in my dreams. I want to feel the rush of air against my face, taste it as it flows through moist ducts and beyond swelling alveoli to nourish a racing heart. If I fall, I'll get right up. Let wounds ooze and weep without worry, for they can be dealt with later. Because right now, I just want to run.

Faster and faster, I want to run, and leave it all in the dust. I want to sprint like Usain Bolt, a bipedal blur, strong and relentless, despite being trapped in a body now withered and bleached and cankered with bedsores. No beckoning cell phone or laptop to slow me down, no IV tubes or dressings or wire leads tethering me down to monitors glowing with jaundice news. If only for a moment or even briefly, I want to run away from the responsibility of being ill; outrun the incessant hemorrhage of bills and pills and insurance forms.

I want to push it beyond the limit, because I know that I can. Leave behind the handicap of fatigue and analgesic and the arthritic solder of chronic disease. I want to run away from life, but I want to live. I want to breathe without the worry of a next coming breath. I want to cry without fear, like tears loosed by the joy of seeing family members triumph. Let those tears paint my cheeks without consequence, in simple brushstrokes of saline, like they did as a child. I want to run and run and run along the floor of the sky, unburdened by the crippling uncertainty and the never-ending question terrorizing my mind—am I going to live or die?

Through whiskered fields or unclean streets, I just want to run—like I once did, like I once could—limbs swinging with the emancipation of youth. Because I know if I could run, nothing else would matter. Because if I could run, I know I could do anything.

An Excerpt from 'Bloody Bill'
by Trularin

Chapter Four

We were at sea for near two months when my mother addressed the cook with a special request. The anniversary of my birth was upon us, a date I keep a constant eye on, and my mother asked the cook to bake a cake, if he could. It was fortunate for us that four live chickens were kept on board for the eggs.

More than once the four of us had heard crewmen talking of a chicken dinner and how great it would be to have such a dinner. However, no one dare touch a single feather, as the captain liked scrambled eggs once a week.

And, as she would have it, the cook agreed to my mother's request. At first, it was a small cake for just our family. The event grew, as my birthday became a point of focus. It wasn't my holiday as much as it was a chance to have a party aboard ship. The cake became a large sheet cake and men began to plan to have time to 'celebrate'.

On the eve of my holiday, my father pulled me aside and blessed me with a bit of knowledge and toasted me with a glass of port he pulled from under his coat.

"Never be afraid of getting the best and you shan't be disappointed." He touched my glass with his. We both drank.

"Bottoms up." I surprised my father. He cocked and eye as if to ask where I might have had used these words before. Hence, he asked.

"The captain toasted our navigation class." I tried to fill his expectations of a grown man in how I answered his question. His reaction was more recognition than surprise as I told him. He dropped his glass into his pocket and waited for me to finish.

The weather had turned warm and it was easy to sport a jacket over a coat. I had mine unbuttoned and open as I drank, maybe a little less formal than my father, I thought, but certainly worthy of the evening air. I stood at the rail and watch out to sea.

The following day found an assortment of events from sleeping in to warm shoes. I was jubilant of the mid-day gathering, to which it appeared the entire ship's complement had joined, to wish me well on this day. For most it was an excuse to relax and enjoy each other without the hard rigger of the ship.

I'm not saying they let the ship adrift, but only the minimal attention was put to the steering and administration of the vessel.

My father, in a stately manner, addressed me before the entire lot and presented me with a brown paper wrapped package and a firm handshake. I looked it over in front of everyone until the captain, of all men, shouted to me to open it.

I grinned and pulled at the wrap quickly and exposed a portion of brass. It was polished and shinny in the sun light. Then, in on final yank, I exposed an eye scope. My jaw dropped in astonishment as I pulled at it to extend it to the fullest.

Putting the great instrument to my eye, I could see everything.

"Dear Lord, its amazing father!" I exclaimed to everyone. In an instant, there was a clamor of merriment and crew members laughed at my announcement. It was to my discovery that someone on board had a violin… and he knew how to play it.

Music drowned the noise of waves bashing the hull of the ship. Men danced, thank God no one sang and my mother and father joined the parents of the other three boys as I displayed my gift with all of its reverence to my comrades.

"May I try it?" Andrew asked. To which I surrendered it to him for a try. He walked towards the edge of the ship and my heart began to pound as I imagined him dropping it by accident over the side.

This was not the case and we all took turns spying various places in the horizon as almost a game to see if one could see better than the other. Of course the scope was only the instrument; there was the factor of interpretation.

"Andy, you're missing the point." Paul argued passing the scope to Daniel. "It wasn't a whale, but a large wave with a cap." Paul finished.

"I say it was a whale. Dan, what do you see?" Andrew asked.

"There is a whale on the horizon, but the waves are also capped. I give both." Daniel settled the disagreement and looked forward.

Equally

by Bruce Reisner

The heat and humidity made the inside of the head seem filled with Crisco. The unpleasantness goes with overheating. It was a bad idea to seek out company on a day like this, like it had been against medical advice. I got on the bus downtown, swearing silently at the thousands of bulging buns-in-the-ovens and thug-like over-inked hides. The tats on people's necks had the threat of Yakuza diluted in the soda pop and slider bus transit. No one all that bad rides the bus, they are simply immune to cheapening and advancement, equally so.

The familiarity of the cultural district worked its wonders in charging contempt, with all the posters of has-beens and second string Broadway actors who come to Pittsburgh like junk mail in black tie. Beneath the posters people line along Heinz Hall waiting for their buses, men and women alike taking turns spitting on the sidewalk and kicking at sparrows hopping on the sidewalks, as if the tiny birds were fouling their vision of urban Hell.

Hiking fast from Penn Avenue to the corner of Liberty and Seventh, I waited with a gang of tattoos and truculent pregnancies. The 14 bus is a new addition to the local fleet, made urgent because of the new casino, which requires daily feeding of souls from all over the region, hence a long and circuitous run. The plan was to take the 14 all the way to Sewickley, the way people take the bus to Fox Chapel. Both places are full of the well-to-do, and both places are rimmed with poor losers who want to make friends there.

They must have saved this particular bus to use on the ride out-bound, because the air conditioning didn't work, though it could be heard wheezing and failing to cool the close air.

As it left the Golden Triangle, pulling off a network of ramps, second thoughts about what I was doing took to nagging. It felt like my mother was pulling me by the arm away from the site of a petty misdeed. The mind began working slightly better than before, and the pointlessness of going to places where people are more affluent began to gel. But the only thing that finalized a decision is that I have a one zone bus pass, and must pay a premium if I take the bus all the way to Sewickley, which reminds me of the word 'sickly,' and is full of vapid rich folks.

Guiltily, I got off in Bellevue, which is a one zone ride. It is just as poor as downtown Pittsburgh, but without the concentration of mean spirit. More guiltily, I walked from the bus stop through and around four blocks of retaining walls and backhoes, to the Red, White and Blue Thrift store, which has been an old vice for many years. After shopping there for nothing, I went across the street to their shiny, brand new Burger King, with its four foot television and its thready WiFi service. Everything in the entire region seems as if it was gifted to humankind by well-meaning communists, and with the smell of fryer grease painting the processed air, with people with their tattooed necks happily munching, feeding French fries to their sallow kids, I decided to forgive people for being what they are. But it's a fast food forgiveness, not to be substituted, too often, for a healthier kind of pardon. The grease in my head will heat again tomorrow.

Unappetizing

by Bruce Reisner

scurry below the flour sack
rodent escapes out the back
stick figure man sets a trap
ghost figure animal laughs
anemic tenant feels like riff-raff
roof rat rolls with mate in the sack
thin horseman of the home goes on attack
tries to clean his filthy digs and lays lilacs
at the hole in the floor the rats come in at
as if they could come to terms

Feel This

by Adrienne S Moody

I heard him before I saw him. I stepped outside and there it was—such a vision of power and beauty. My son sat in its driver's seat and looked at me, proud and excited—his new toy. It was a Camaro Z28 sporting a T-bar roof, standard, with 375 horses under the hood.

Oh my god.

"Get in, Mom!" I did and marveled at the sound of the engine sounding anxious to break out of the gates. "Ready?" he warned and I nodded.

He took me out on a quieter road and opened it up. He's learned how to double clutch and downshift to get the most out of the powerful engine. We grinned at each other. The day was warm, mid-summer.

"This is the most powerful car I've been in since your dad and I owned that canary yellow Firebird with a 450 Hurst shifter!"

He looked at me like I challenged him.

"Oh yeah! FEEL THIS!!!" and he dropped the gear and floored the gas pedal. The monster was out of the cage and one hand grabbed the sissy bar and the other his shoulder, which I squeezed.

What a ride.

He dropped me back off at my car, sitting so demurely and domesticated. I said goodbye to him as he drove off, so happy, my son. He was in possession of his dream car. He told me that when he first got it he took an exit off the freeway and floored it. The car went sideways and he thought, "I love it..."
I went home and later on in bed my eyes blinked in the darkness.

I couldn't sleep.

...be careful, my son... you like speed far too much... please don't drink and take this wildcat out on the highway... please... please... be careful...

I made a mental note to text him the next day and tell him that i had a terrible dream about him and his Camaro.

He knows all about my dreams and how some of them do come true.

I thought of when I taught him how to drive. I took him on a country road and told him to turn off and turn himself around. He did and looked at me unexpectedly. Okay...I said .... I know you're going to do burnouts, so show me now if you can do it safely. He looked at me with fire in his eyes. Really? He asked. Really I confirmed. We waited for traffic to clear and he gunned my little 6 cylinder and we side winded onto the road spitting gravel behind us. Okay, okay, okay, I remember saying. Wow I didn't expect that. I thought afterward, I know the boy can handle a car just like his dad did.

Sweet Grass
by Gaboo

I can't write about her now, not at this moment. The act would take pages. I need to be somewhere large and open, where grasses meet sky. Then I can find the air and the room to remember. A summer? We were sitting, leaning backs to a fence, plucking stories and grass, hanging on words, ears wide to each other's cue. We were submerged and innocent.

She was talking, or smirking, telling puns and I was so close, casual close and friendship comfortable—when the touch of a finger or a brush against cloth was everything. Her nose was sunburned, like mine, and she had parched lips and a loose gap in her teeth. One lip, the top, was too thin and the bottom one always looked swollen. She had an odd face, with heavy eyebrows, and eyes for finding mischief. She was mesmerizing, swift and beautiful.

I keep coming back to that time, out at the fence, where we relaxed one afternoon and chewed grass, talking and kidding. That's when I caught the glint of sweat on her temple. Soaked wisps and strands fell over her ear and trailed back to her cheek.

This was profound! She was sweating! Girls don't sweat? I had to know if she had a smell—like shoes, or paint, or butter. I listened to her, giggling and going on and on. And while she talked, I inhaled, gently, so careful not to breathe on her neck. She smelled of mosquito repellent, barn straw, dirt and sweet grass. Freedom and sweet grass.

Breaking Camp

by Steven Bird

(Mature: some coarse language)

It was almost dark when he arrived. He'd driven straight through all the way from Massachusetts without sleeping. He said the Badlands made him thirsty. Soon as he crossed into Montana Richard stopped and bought two bottles of Jack Daniels. Pounded a whole fifth while driving across the Big Sky and Idaho panhandle. Cracked open the second bottle as soon as he hit camp. He said he hadn't come to fish.

Gary helped him polish off the rest of the whiskey around the fire while Richard played Al DiMeola full volume on the camp stereo. "…Listen to that… wait… listen to that…" he said, holding a finger up, nodding and smiling like he was sharing the sweetest revelation, then he danced, a stumbling dancing bear swaying dangerously close to falling into the fire. "I love you Cuz," he kept saying, earnest and fierce, "I love you Cuz."

The fire died down to coals. Gary and I decided to call it a night. We tried to get Richard to bed in one of the cabin tents I reserve for clients who've come to fish, but he refused to go into the tent. He lurched away into the outer dark and fell down over

214

by the boat shed. We hauled him into the shed and dumped him on an air mattress.

He managed to poke a hole in the mattress and woke up on the floor at five in the morning still drunk on his ass, and wanting to fish. He pulled over the rack we store the fishing rods on, about twenty rods left scattered and tangled on the floor. Couldn't find his shoes, but he found the box of winter boots and dumped them all out on top of the rods. He selected a pair of giant, white, arctic boots that I use for ice fishing and pulled them on; then he found my favorite rod and took off down to the river, where he fell face-first down the rocky embankment.

Scraped his nose and raised a big goose egg on his forehead and broke the middle finger of his right hand. Busted the tip off my best rod and scratched the reel all to hell. I drove him to the clinic in Northport where they splinted the middle finger straight, creating a permanent flip-off gesture of his hand. Rich talked the doctor into writing him a prescription for a month's supply of strong oxycodins. Outside the clinic he turned a full circle on the sidewalk dancing a little jig, a banged up fat guy, his shaved head a crazy jack-o-lantern with the front teeth broken out from other falls, his hand raised high, saluting the shabby little river town with the big finger, "We're still numba one!" he called out, "We're still numba one!"

On the way back from town Richard opened up. "See what's happenin Cuz? I keep hurting myself. I get so fucked up. The stroke fucked me up. I nevah drank whiskey before the stroke. It's the only thing that makes me not give a fuck about what it did to me. That an the pills. The fuckin doctahs got me hooked on pills. I can't do nothin. Can't work. Can't ride my motorcycle. Can't get a hard on. Can't even cast a fishing rod anymore. I'm retahdid. It's like bein retahdid Cuz."

I'm a guide. An outfitter. I take people fishing. Bird watching. Float down the river. I am not a qualified therapist. Oh, I do okay with horses, animals, but I've never claimed to be able to put broken people back together again. Barely keeping myself together. But everybody's got some crosses to bear, I guess. I had Gary and Richard for the summer, and the family was counting on me to get them squared away. My mother insisted I take Gary on. Then Richard's wife Cathy and my uncle and cousins in the East took turns calling to prep me for Richard's visit. He'd already been through rehab five times and failed to detox every time. Cathy and his little girl came home one day, and there he was, passed out in a heap at the bottom of a stairway, his head in a pool of blood. Fell down. Drunk. Cathy was desperate. She called me: "…Stevie you are my last hope. Rich looks up to you. This is his last chance. If he can't get off the pills and booze out

216

theyah with you I'm gonna have to let him go Steve, I'm going to let him go. I can't have Nikki seeing him like that all the time."

My brother Gary, by himself, wasn't too bad. Gary is a conspiracy theorist who needs only the smallest of openings to launch into a rambling, rapid-fire diatribe against the Zionist-Jew plan for world domination. His slide toward living in a tent out at my camp began last year during a nasty break-up with his wife: He left a death threat message on her cellphone. She played it for the cops. When they caught up with him there was a loaded shotgun riding in the pickup. They charged him with a felony: making a terrorist threat. And having a loaded gun in a vehicle. The loaded shotgun weighed heavy in the judge's decision, even though Gary had no prior record. He spent his last dollar fighting it. The judge gave him six months solid. Nobody in the family had the money to cover his land and truck payments and he lost everything while he was in jail. He couldn't keep his mouth shut in County and got seriously thumped a couple of times by the guards and once by another inmate. Spent almost the entire term in solitary confinement. He's plenty broken alright. But everything else aside, he is unfailingly loyal to me. I can handle him. He seemed to be making good progress wrestling with his demons on his own. I wasn't too worried about him. He's a pretty good cook, so I gave him a job as camp cook for the season. He was doing okay. But cousin Richard was another case.

217

I've known some people with bad addictions, but I've never seen a jones like the one Richard had for the combination of whiskey and pain pills. He'd always been a partier, but ever since the stroke froze half his face and ended his sales career a couple years ago, he'd gotten worse with the prescription painkillers. The second day of his stay, a couple of clients arrived, a nice couple from Pennsylvania. They'd booked me to take them flyfishing on the river and they were going to camp with us for three days. Turned out they were drinkers, and they let us know on their first night that they'd brought a good supply of expensive Scotch single malt. Richard latched onto them and downed most of their supply while entertaining them with stories from our childhood on the lake in Mass: "Hey Stevie rememba that time we were fishin, and you weren't lookin where you were castin and put that Bass-O-Reno in Pauly Reagan's head? All three treble hooks. Stevie was a holy terra. Crazy fuck, weren't ya?... You know you were." And also: "Rememba that time we pitched a tent out in the back yard? Stole my dad's Playboy and jerked to the pictures half the night. Goddamn crazy fucks."

Ah god. I couldn't even look at the woman after that. Gary followed Richard's lead and got in on the whiskey, too, and his mouth got loose: "…When are you people gonna wake up? Don't you know that the Jews are running everything? Huh? What's it gonna take to make you realize that?..."

After the clients left I read Gary and Richard the Riot Act. They were not to mingle with my clients. They were to keep their conversations with the paying guests down to a polite minimum. They were not to drink alcoholic beverages or take dope of any kind while they stayed at the camp. The talk served as a temporary gut-check for Gary, and had no effect on Richard at all.

End of his first week at camp: Richard was out of money and out of gas. He spent eight hundred bucks driving the ten miles to town twice a day for beer and whiskey, and he'd gone through the entire month's prescription of oxies. I suspected that he was sharing them with Gary. By the second day of oxies: they'd degenerated into two shuffling and unblinking manatees, drifting through the trees between their tents and the refrigerator in the boat shed for beer; Richard's Al DiMeola collection blasting from the screen room at the center of camp. I had a couple of clients over from Seattle, a couple of English teachers, and at the end of their second day, after fishing, one of them comes to me and says: "I think that guy Rich is taking beer out of our cooler... I wouldn't care that much... except he drank it all, all we brought to last us the week..."

Out of money, gas and pills, Richard was on the hustle. He bummed enough money from Gary to get to town for a bottle of whiskey. Without the pills he needed to drink more to achieve the required buzz. He drank the entire fifth in his tent; then pulled the tent down on himself, breaking the tent-poles. He freaked because he couldn't find the opening, so he got out his pocket knife and cut a hole through the roof big enough to ride a horse through and ruined my seven hundred dollar Alaskan Guide cabin tent.

I had to do something about Richard. The family was counting on me. And Richard was counting on me, I knew, because every time he got good and whacked he'd get to a point he'd start crying about how he had to quit the booze and pills, and how it was killing him, and how he was going to lose Cathy and the kids if he didn't kick. And then his mood would switch to: "Aw fuck it, I don't give a fuck."

So much for good intentions.

I hatched a plan. Luckily I didn't have any clients around who might be frightened, so I was free to get creative. Self-help wasn't working for Richard. He'd thought the change of scenery alone would be the catharsis he needed. The stillness of isolation is like a still pond and acts as a mirror, and whatever it was Richard was seeing in that mirror he was not able to confront on his own.

He was sleeping it off in the cheapo dome tent we set up for him after he ruined the big one. I fetched twenty feet of anchor chain and a couple of padlocks out of the boat shed and crept over to the tent. I padlocked one end of the chain around a pine by the tent opening, and then, slowly, unzipped the door enough to reach in with the chain and padlock it around Richard's left ankle. Then I went and told Gary about it.

"Are you nuts? You can't leave him chained to a tree. You're crazy. What's he gonna shit and piss in?"

"Five gallon bucket. He's staying there until I say he's done. We'll bring him food and empty the bucket. And make sure he doesn't get any booze. Okay?"

"… Aw shit… you're serious?"

"Yep."

"…Well… okay… But if he dies it's on you man. Right?"

"Sure," I said, "I'll take the blame if he dies."

See. When you train a horse, the first thing you do is tie the horse to a strong post with a stout rope. If you leave the horse tied there long enough it will eventually become tractable. Like I said, I'm not a qualified therapist. Hard for me to articulate the change that takes place in a horse's brain as a result of the tying. Let's just say that the process rearranges some synapses in the horse's head, and the horse comes out of it with a healthy respect for the rope. You can't use the rope alone to master the horse because the horse is a lot stronger than you. You just tie him up, then stand back. At first the horse will fight. Maybe fight for a long time. But in every case the horse will eventually tire of struggling against the immovable post and stand quietly. You let the rope and the post and time do the work. When the horse is standing completely relaxed, head down, ears down, you walk over and untie the rope from the post, and the horse thinks you're his best friend for it. A light pull on the rope and he follows. Until Richard, I had never tried this on a human.

Richard woke up. When he swung his feet off the cot the chain jingled and he looked down. He clambered outside the tent tracing his tether to the pine. "You bastids. Ha-ha. Funny. Now c'mon, get this chain off me, I gotta take a shower," he called across the camp.

I brought a bucket of warm water, washcloth, soap and a towel, set it down by his tent. "Here you go Cuz."

A smile edged its way across his face. "C'mon Steve, unlock the chain, quit fuckin aroun."

"Nope. Sorry Richard. This is it man. Now's your chance to really do it. We're leaving you here until you're done." Then I turned and walked away.

Richard lurched after me. "Hey come on... you aint serious..." He almost tripped when the chain clinked tight as he reached for my shoulder. "Oh boy... you fuckin fuck. You mothafuckin fuckin fuck..." Then he spit at me.

He didn't sleep for the first four days. At night he howled like a wolf and laughed and cried. Strange voices came from his tent in the dark. One, like a child talking baby-talk that I couldn't make out. Sometimes he'd yell in a plaintive voice, "JESUS! JESUS! JESUS!" Then there was this wicked, cackling voice that said cryptic things like: "You can't do that. Never. No never. You know you can't do that. That. That. That." I could see how these things might be interpreted as demonic possession. But I figured the voices were just the various problems surfacing in his brain and being released through his vocal chords. Like toxins sweated out in a sauna. He threw the plate at me the first time I tried to bring him food, so I had Gary attend to him. Richard knew it was my idea, and that I held the keys to the padlock, so he wasn't nearly as pissed at Gary as he was at me. He raised a ruckus for the first four days though.

He was able to sleep by the fifth day. That was a relief to us all. He spent most of the time sleeping after that. Gary brought him a pad of drawing paper and a pencil.

On the sixth day, I went over to check on him. I half expected him to grab me and choke me out with the chain as soon as I came within reach, but was surprised to find him fairly resigned to his situation.

"I'm hurtin, man. This is hell," he said without moving from the cot.

I noticed the sketchbook beside him, an entire page covered with sketches of eyes. Just eyes with eyebrows. They were the saddest eyes I've ever seen, perfectly rendered in various expressions of torment and sorrow. "I didn't know you are an artist. Those are good. Ever thought about taking an art class? Might meet some people there you have something in common with. Might be a good way to track your life on to something less apt to kill you."

"Maybe I'll do that. Thought about it. I'm done drinkin Cuz. I'm done. You can let me off the chain now. Let me off the chain."

I thought about it. He looked so pathetic. But he did look a little healthier. "I'm thinking about it," I told him as I walked away.

I left Richard chained to the tree for six more days. The chain accomplished what five expensive stays at various institutions could not. He detoxed.

By the time I unlocked Richard's chain the season was almost over. I was heading down to California in a few days. Gary was staying on at camp until he could put a better situation together for himself. The engine in his car burned up so I was leaving him my pickup. Richard had never seen the redwoods and was looking forward to driving me down the coast. We spent the last few days breaking camp. Pitched horseshoes. Richard and I fished in the evenings. He didn't say anything about wanting a drink and seemed to be doing okay.

The night was exquisite and the stars were very close, driving south from Crescent City. Broken plumes of fog from over the Pacific rose up like whale ghosts against the Del Norte headlands. We needed to get some sleep. I pulled off onto a wide shoulder beside a grove of big trees. We rolled our sleeping bags out on the ground, and we laid side by side, looking up at the patchwork of starry sky knitted to inkblot crowns of tall redwoods assembled around us like giants in the dark. They drink hundreds of gallons of water a day. At night the trees drip. And the pure drops distilled through their millennial bodies fell on us like tears through the night.

Our sleeping bags were soaked through by first light. We packed up and hit the road, needing coffee, the car heater blasting us dry.

The morning fog departed under the breaking sun. We rolled slow down the Redwood Highway through deep shadow then spotted light beneath the boughs. I drove while Richard looked out the window contemplating the ranks of ancient trees.

"I love you Cuz. You know that, right? I know some crazy bastids, but you're probably the only one nuts enough to chain me to a tree."

"Yeah. Probably."

"What do you figure my chances of makin it are?"

"… Oh, fifty-fifty? Sure. I suppose anybody has a fifty-fifty chance of making it," I said, not really knowing, but hoping it was so. "We just do our best. That's all we can do, I guess. We just try to do our best."

Oso's Berry Good Day
by Sheila Cano

Had a late start to the berry picking today. Noodling on the internet, going to the library, shopping in the neighbourhood, treating myself to a lunch of wonton soup and Szechuan green beans with pork. Set out (after leaving word with a friend) for Mt. Seymour late in the afternoon. Armed with insect repellent, first aid kit, emergency kit (compass, headlamp, matches, lighter, space blanket, whistle, forgot the Swiss army knife). Got up there at the indecent hour of 6pm, just in time for the evening cloud of no-see-ums. Tinier than skeeters but their bite flares up like a black fly. Already nursing two or three bites from earlier in the week.

Found a good berry patch only minutes from the car, on Goldie Hill. It's the bunny slope in the ski season, so the berry bushes are short. I look for the ones that are turning purple already - those are the black bilberries, my favorites. Ask Ellie, she's sampled them, sweeter than the 'blue'-berries. I place my pack on the ground and wander around from bush to bush, picking the biggest berries I can find. They fill the bucket quicker

227

than the small ones do. After half an hour, I have half a litre (quart to you US folks).

I hear a snort, kind of like a horse. I look up, and about a half a block away there is my namesake, another Sheila Cano. The black bear is noshing on berries, unconcerned with my presence.

Not wishing to get into a turf war which I cannot win, I wander slowly back to my packsack, stash the berry container and hoist the pack. Walk slowly away uphill, keeping an eye on oso2. Take my camera out, and zoom in for a shot (still looks like a little black dot, that far away). Oso2 wanders into the forest and disappears.

I meander up the hill to a berry patch closer to the parking lot. En route, a raven hops around the picnic area, looking for scraps no doubt. S/he poses for a photo. Continuing my berry quest, I find myself spending as much time swatting no-see-ums as picking berries. Finally I give up as 7:30 approaches, and head back to the car. A woman waiting by her car while her partner uses the washroom tells me they saw smoke down the hill, and a helicopter.

Partway along the road, the smoke thickens, and I come to a stop behind several other vehicles. Two fire trucks are at the bend

228

in the road, smoke billowing above them. A traffic coordinator with fluorescent safety vest holds us back while the fire is subdued. People get out of their cars, walk their dogs, watch the scene. I realize I'm going to be late getting home, and ask a young man if I can use his cell phone to call my friend, so she won't worry about me. The sun is setting and it's nearing 8pm. He shows me a picture he's taken with his phone, of a shiny red pickup truck with the engine on fire, before the fire trucks arrived.

Finally the smoke clears, and we are allowed to pass by the gutted vehicle. Just a blackened shell is left. The sky is vivid with sunset clouds. The trip home is somehow surreal, and for once I keep to the speed limit while contemplating the events of the day.

The Dreaming Garden
by Sheila Cano

Alona pushed loose tendrils of hair behind her ears. The wind picked up, and she drew her sweater close as she looked at the garden. Summer had passed, leaving drying stems and withering leaves. The pea vines were overcome with powdery mildew and the last tomatoes lingered on the yellowing stalks. Weeds carpeted the paths between rows of vegetables. Another season, another harvest, and not everything she had planted had thrived.

In one corner, separated by a line of abalone shells, was her dreaming garden. This spring she had planted buttons, hoping to grow a new dress. Last year, she sowed some locks of her own hair, which was thinning now and turning grey. Many years ago she planted a pair of men's shoes. Each year she made a wish as she dug in her dreaming garden. Yet nothing ever grew, except weeds.

Alona Fortune, what a name to bear, she thought. All during her teaching career, the children had called her "Miss Fortune." Someone in the back row usually snickered, and she would glare at him until he stopped grinning and folded his hands on the desk.

Now that she had retired, she missed seeing the children each day. She even missed the ones who laughed behind her back.

She began turning over the soil, digging the weeds under. At least they would sprout next year, bearing colourful flowers of pink clover, purple vetch and yellow dandelions. Her trowel hit something hard. She dug deeper, uncovering a small wooden box. Her heart pounded as the memory came back, the day she had sowed this dream. She brushed the dirt off the box and pried it open with the trowel. Inside was a pair of baby booties. Alona began to weep.

As her tears dried, she resolved to plant a bottle of sleeping pills next spring. Why wait? she thought, I'll go get them now. She walked back to her house, carefully scraping her shoes on the hedgehog brush beside the door. In the bathroom, she rummaged among her medications and found what she wanted. She went back outside with the bottle of barbiturates, and put it in the hole where the wooden box had been. As she covered it with soil she said to herself, it's time, it may as well be time.

She went into the house again, to put away the trowel and change out of her gardening clothes. As she took off her work shirt, she saw a brand-new dress hanging in the closet. It was white, covered with pale lilac flowers. Alona felt her insides begin to churn, and every hair on her body lifted in a sizzle of emotion. She put her work shirt back on, grabbed the trowel, and ran to her dreaming garden.

Farm Life

by Adrienne S Moody

Growing up I visited my Uncle's farms in Northern Alberta during summer vacation. This is what I think of when I bike the Mud Bay Trail which on one side the ocean is always (it seems) in low tide format, and on the other side are farmer's fields. I am drawn to the bike path every summer. During the wintry wet months I pass by a small portion of it on the highway and I always take a wistful glance.

The prairies never leave someone who grew up there. We may never want to move back to the flat lands but a part of us aches for the big sky at sunset and the golden waves of wheat in the hot summer sun. We hear a roll of thunder in our transplanted home and we will recall that violent crash of thunder and golf ball size hail of the prairie. Nothing smells like the first splatter of rain on hot dry soil.

My Uncle Victor had an interesting face, the face of a farmer cracked deeply by sun exposure and skin around his eyes crinkled like rice paper, from constant searching the horizon for changes in the weather. I would sit at the breakfast table across from this

233

giant of a man and watch him move the toothpick around his mouth without touching it. He didn't speak during this time of day, already toiled a couple hours in the barn with milking the cows...back then it was all done by hand and he had thirty head of cattle and four strapping sons to help. If he was asked a question by his wife, he'd answer but his eyes never left the constant watch of the skies.

He was my hero.

One spring he motioned for me to follow him to the back of the barn and I obeyed, carefully stepping around cow pies.

"Look," he pointed ten or so feet away and then I saw it. A calf just born stood shakily on its feet. Its coat looked shiny and gooey and I watched fascinated as the mother licked him and he found its source of nourishment within minutes and sucked greedily. "See, it's the only animal I know of that learns all it needs to learn in life in only a few minutes after birth."

He would show me all the hiding places that his chickens would use to hide their eggs. This was the one chore they trusted me to do and I checked hourly. It was like hunting for treasure. I loved the feel of the warmth of the eggs. One time I couldn't get a chicken to budge and I knew there was an egg under her, so I called my cousin Ralph, a rangy kid with blond hair and a

234

chipped tooth. He smiled wickedly at me and said, "I'll fix that little problem," and re-entered the chicken coop with a short whip and whipped the poor creature.

She moved and I never asked him for help again.

One time I dropped an egg on the porch and it splattered messily and my Aunt scolded me like it was gold. I learned to be more careful.

I will never forget the strong smell of manure and spoiled milk. I treasure the sight of the darkness like no other and the stars crowding the sky with brilliant light. The kind of dark that you can't see your hand in front of you.

I wanted my husband to be a farmer when we first married. I pleaded. He finally in exasperation said, "I'm not a farmer, Ellie. Understand that: I'm never going to be a farmer."

It was a sad day for me, but he was right. I would miss my thrift stores, and restaurants, and Starbucks. I would miss the lights from the city, I suppose. But every time I pass my Mud Bay Park in my car speeding down the highway at 100 kilometers, my eyes drink in the path that I know borders on farmers fields and I can visualize the corn stalks tall in the autumn bending with the ocean breeze.

Watersports

by Gaboo

(Mature: some coarse language)

I see Eeyore sitting at the bench next to the lagoon. It's midday, Friday, and not much going on at the park. People are working. There's a few yoga types and couple mom sets herding kids near the beach. I call him Eeyore when he looks depressed. He is an E. Orr. Ensen Orr. I think I'm the only one that gave him the nickname though, and I think it bothered him originally, but he gets it now. He's my neighbor's kid.

He's wearing joggers and jeans, rumpled orange T, and two soldiers in a six pack parked on his lap. Day off, I guess. So I sidle up.

"Your mom called our house."

He's gazing across a bike path into a pond. Bullrushes clump around a little pristine divot, except where we're sitting, the only viewpoint, a patch of soggy grass covered in goose paste. He takes a swig and kicks gravel.

"Yeah, thanks," he says.

"You just hangin' out?"

"Yeah."

"I'm headin' back uptown—"

"Maybe, after this."

"Well, I'll wait around."

Eeyore fidgets and kicks more gravel. He's getting antsy, me sitting here. The scenery's nice, peaceful, a little watercolor. Ducks drift in trios at the far end.

"Gotta smoke?" he asks, fixated on the water.

"Buy your own."

He almost looks surprised, eyebrows go up, but he doesn't look at me, instead smirks and says, "Nice guy."

"I don't have any."

Eeyore slumps again, yanks a can and nods it at me.

"Na," I answer.

He sets the beer on the bench between us and pulls the last one from the six-pack tabs, puts the can on his other side and then flicks the polyethylene scrap sideways from shoulder height. The plastic rings plane air and clear the grass, ditching in the murk about arm's length offshore. He stares at the launch, holding his follow through, then he's "Hrmmf", like he could have done better.

I instinctively look back and forth along the bike path. Half a jog away, there's some villager walking towards us—capri's, fashion ballcap, lulu-eco shopping bag. I already know she's a Noreen and sits on a committee. I've never met her.

"Where'd you get the beer?" I ask him.

"Bought it."

"Right." I start playing kick-the-gravel game, too.

"It was in a car up there," he thumbs over his shoulder, behind us to the parking lot, "Just sittin' there goin' to waste. Gettin' hot—some stupid ass."

Eeyore gawks at his personal pollution, slowly moving adrift, but I'm watching the watcher. I know she's gearing up, because she's marching now, getting closer and her fists are clenching.

"Why don't you get a milf?" he blurts, leaning back, eyes off among the fowl, paddling in their little viridian serenity.

"I don't really know what that is."

He's squinting, like he's trying to put the definition in a simpler package.

"A mother," he finally says, sparing my sensitivities.

"Where'd you learn that one?"

"Ah, I hear Rob call Mom that all the time."

Rob's his mom's boyfriend. I'm thinking about what Eeyore just said when a five-foot-eight, forty-year-old woman intent on something pulls up puffing. She looks over at the pond—sublime, really, except for Eeyore's eyesore—and then back to the two of us. She stares, like we're culprits.

"I saw what you did," she huffs. For some reason, I know she's tried to put a cat on a leash.

"Did what?" Eeyore counters, defiant.

"You threw that in there," she points with her left eye at Eeyore and then at the plastic ringlette.

"So what?" he challenges, flat line. She drops her head lower and peers out from the rim of her ball cap. She has blue gray eyes that catch reflections, captivating, but her eyebrows look stitched on. I'd call her casual prim.

"What do mean, 'So what?'" Then she looks at me, "Aren't you going to tell him to pick that up?"

I shrug and droop my mouth, innocent bystander here.

She continues into me, "You should make him pick that up! Gee, that's great parenting."

"He's not my kid."

That took her off a bit, but she rallies, "Then set an example. Tell him he shouldn't do that."

I know she works with books. I speak slowly, "I haven't had a chance yet."

She's just marched sixty paces looking for a fight. I don't think she's done.

"Do you know the damage that can do?" she says, going directly at the perp. I'm shaking my head, giving her my best concerned citizen signal so she'll forget about me.

"No," Eeyore answers her.

"When you throw those things in there, ducks can get trapped and strangle, and die—." She throttles the last syllable for dramatic effect.

Eeyore's still looking at the woman, his head cocked, nose scrunched, eyes squinting against back light, trying to distinguish her attitude like he's been ordered to classify a new vegetable.

"Well, don't you understand?" Her eyes open wide and she rolls her head back and forth. It's the communicating with the learning disabled stance. She continues, slower, "When you throw your garbage in there, it can hurt the little duckies."

Eeyore frowns and speaks, "I think you're full of crap."

She didn't expected him to say that. Her fluster upticks. Then Eeyore juts out, "You've never seen a dead duck from a six pack ring, have you?"

She's on defense, "I don't have to see one, everybody knows that can happen."

"Who says?"

"Everybody. The park people, the TV, the news—you should know that. Besides, you're littering!"

"I throw six pack rings in there all the time. I never caught a duck."

"Are you serious?" Her lecture's gone astray; kid's too complex, "You shouldn't even be drinking!"

"I shouldn't be talking to strange freaks."

Both parties digress.

"Well, then—you're just a mean brat. You're going to get a fine."

"Well, you're full of crap."

An impasse, I'm shutting up.

Her bag's heavy, she plunks it on the path. A mini puff of chalk earth erupts as it lands. We haven't had rain for weeks, though muggy today. People are testy.

"Are you going to pick up your garbage?" she's challenging Eeyore. I'm not sure if she intends to drag him to the water.

"No," he snips. I could have told her he's a button pusher, but she "Hrummfs", whirls and marches across the soggy grass to water's edge. Her footsteps go spluck. She surveys the little floating death trap just out of reach, and begins problem-solving,

242

then fiddles with the nearest, dry bullrush stock, and snaps it from the shoot.

"Hey, you shouldn't do that," Eeyore calls out, "that's destroying nature!"

She spins a stare back at him, "It was already dead."

She changes her approach and begins stepping gingerly, so as not to disrupt some rare nesting grounds. Spluck, spluck. Her Hi-tecs withdraw with an ominous vacuum.

She's approaching her quarry in full stance, right arm maneuvering outwards. She's got the reed by the brown bull cap, left arm cantilevered behind her. It's a good fencing pose. However, the bog's not up to the pressure—even lawnmower guy left the last pass unkempt. She makes one brisk parry and the shoreline sinks. I wince. I can feel the water fill up her sneaker.

"Shit!"

"Are you alright?"

"Yes! I'm alright—I just got my foot soaked!"

There's no way to pull out from her position. The mud's got her forward foot. In a heroic display, the other shoe leaps to it's sib's aid and plants shin deep in the ditch water. She's committed now and should have worn Crocs.

Again, doors open on the hinges of serendipity, and a guy, Beau Studly, her male doppelganger, is walking past, slowing, watching us watching her, looking at her like she's a bag lady fishing empties. He's a healthy buck, ear tagged with a Bluetooth.

"She's teachin' us how to catch ducks," comments Eeyore.

"I am not!" she yells back, almost losing her balance, "I'm cleaning up your garbage!"

She whips the reed around to wave it at Eeyore and catches glimpse of Beau framed in silver birch vignette, a Ray Ban sire with full shroud upon the mantle, blackberry in his sword arm, flying colors of her same dominion on his own hemp fiber eco bag.

"That brat is tossing garbage in the pond," she sneers at Eeyore.

Beau gears down, approaching a sideshow car wreck in his invisible beemer.

She points her baton at Eeyore, assuring everyone can identify the miscreant, but we're all looking at her. Suddenly the stalk cracks, right at the tang, drooping to the soup like a dowsing rod. I know Beau's switching apps, thinking YouTube.

The plastic flotsam is another step out. Provided the silt isn't too deep, she might as well grab her prey and slog back. She decides same, and takes another prod forward. Everyone's mistake who thought that would work. Balance lost, she knows that in a moment, forward is a face plant. So, backwards she goes.

It's a quality slow motion entry and even the ducks take off. Her capris are done—I'm thinking there's always MasterCard.

"Ooh, that sucks—" Eeyore can't contain his good fortune.

"You prick!" She yells at him.

"Hey, he's a kid," I apprise her.

Beau finds the app.

"You turn that stupid thing off!" She jams her hands in the muck and rolls up on one knee, where she can stand. She wrings her hands and swacks the dredge off her pants, then trudges another two steps deeper and plucks Eeyore's plastic doily.

Beau tucks his handbag under his sword arm and extends the other. He's gesturing the air between them closer. He won't approach the bank. She marches up the turf past him and stands on the bike path in front of Eeyore, draining, then turns on a heel and thrusts the ringlette into the waste can at the far end of the rest stop.

"You should recycle," says Eeyore. It's like a twitch—he can't resist. I guess at that age you figure you can move faster.

She strides back to her shopping bag on the gravel, "Hrummf," and stands as a martyr to dignity. But Beau's moving closer, expression aghast. Eeyore and I lean closer. She follows our horrified gaze, and I think she knows it before she looks down. There's a leech moored to her knee. I give her credit, she's braver than I and ball-peens it with her forefinger. The mud sucker splats on the gravel and writhes.

Where it was hinged to her body, a small trickle of blood oozes and blends with the swamp sluice.

Eeyore scrunches his nose and squints, "I think I'm gonna puke."

Even Beau recoils.

Our eco-warrior looks spent. She made a valiant effort and maybe saved a life. I don't know how that works. Chivalry gets the best of Beau and he scoops the handles on her bag, "Are you alright? I can walk you back uptown?"

"No, thanks!" She yanks the bag away and eyes the long slog up the bike path. Beau shrugs and struts off, cutting through the park. Shame, they might have got on any other day.

"Let's go to the beach," I announce to Eeyore. I don't want to, but we can detour in the opposite direction and head back up along the boardwalk.

"Sure." says Eeyore. He pushes the full can into his front pocket, walks to the trash and plops in his empties.

He turns, looking at his sodden combatant and in an earnest grumble, cedes, "Sorry, lady. You win. That was bonus."

Sugar Snaps
by M Dawn Thacker

Grandma and Grandpa used to sit on the front porch shelling peas. Grandpa went to the garden and picked. Everyone shelled. I called myself "helping". It seemed to take hours to shell those peas. I'd pop open the end of a pod, run my fingernail down the crease between the halves and scatter out five to six peas into the white enamel colander, the one with the red ring around the edge. Those little green balls rolled around in the bottom of that colander for a long time before we shelled a "mess". Sometimes, there were eight peas to the pod, on a rare occasion there were nine, and once, I remember eleven. Grandma and Grandpa talked about that particular pod until the butterbeans came in. "You remember that pea pod with eleven?" Grandma would ask.

"Yep," Grandpa said, "eleven, hard to believe. I remember one time when I was a kid, we opened one with thirteen, never matched that one."

Our sugar snaps are in now. We planted the seeds at the end of February and have watched them sprout, climb and bloom. On Saturday we gathered a handful, thinking there wouldn't be much of a crop. I was sad because they are my favorites and I look forward to them in the spring. Last year by this time, we had put up freezer bags full.

On the way home tonight, the sky was full of storm. Clouds puffed and billowed to the West. The heat and humidity hung around my shoulders when I got out of the car. I had clothes on the line and wanted them in before the shower. I heard thunder as I unclipped the towels, washcloths and tee shirts.

When storms gather clouds, dark with wind and rain, everything on the ground seems brighter. The sugar snaps caught my eye, their blooms, extra white, their vines that bright spring green. I hurried over to the garden and found pods hanging, ready to be picked. I ran inside and traded the clothes basket for the colander.

I don't like thunderstorms, never have. I've dragged boys off baseball fields, run from the beach, leaving bags, umbrellas and sand shovels behind, and stayed in my car for half an hour to wait out the lightning rather than dash into the house. Today, thunder rumbled and I stayed in the garden to pick. I was quick about it, keeping an eye to the distance. I hadn't seen lightning, and the rain was holding off. As I rounded one row and started back toward the gate, picking the other, the first fat drop of rain fell. I kept gathering. The booms of thunder were coming closer, and then the distance lit up with lightning. I left my row and ran back to the house as the rain began in earnest.

I had the white enamel colander full of peas. Having purchased my grandparent's house in the mid-eighties affords me the luxury of sitting on their front porch. I took the peas there and sat in Grandma's rocker to wait for the storm and my family to arrive.

You don't shell sugar snap peas. You snap off the stem and bloom ends and pop them right into your mouth. That's what I like about them, they're quick and easy. There's no time for all that sitting and shelling these days, what with forty-hour work weeks, children to haul to sports and school events, and sleep to catch up on.

For now, sugar snaps are perfect. Maybe when I retire, I'll plant some Alderman peas; those are the seeds my Grandpa sowed. I can sit on his front porch and teach my grandchildren how to shell a "mess" of peas, tell a good story, and dream of finding that elusive "thirteen" peas in one pod.

Fruit Fly

by Bruce Reisner

some protein in little bodies

and no germ can survive the chemical spirits

the infestation of fruit flies is unbeatable

I surrender to the itch by drinking whiskey

and the flies annoy me

rim the shot glass like salt

fruit flies

the salt of the Earth

sit on the rim of a shot glass

and fall into the acid

they taunted me and died in the whiskey

I see their corpse in the whiskey

drink them

honor them

see determination in amber and drink it

Looking Back
by Sarah Scott

Spaghetti smeared across beige walls,
little feet skip through unlit halls,
wistful sketches in my mind
stored away for me to find
years later,
when they're all grown up.

I'm staring into a medicine cup
filled with pills to slow the cancer.
The doctor awaits my answer.
Do I want to spend my days like this?
I shake my head and recount past bliss,
swaddled in a child's smile
and loves embrace.

Those treasures come back to me;
they light up my face,
and eclipse the pain
searing through my limbs.
In my mind I'm dancing to his whims,

soaking up his smell;
all is well.

They're gathered 'round my hospital bed,
recounting tales while I'm fed
another round of pills to stay the pain.
A silken voice whispers in my ear,
my little Jane, and I recall angelic curls
and deep green eyes,
nights spent soothing brokenhearted cries.

My precious family all around,
and I'm unable to utter a simple sound.
The pain grows sharper now,
and I see him there, guiding me somehow,
holding my hand
through hazy moments.

My nostrils fill with their scents,
and then they're gone,
whisked away with faces all somber
and shades of gray.
Caught up in visions,
I passed today.

Elbows In Jam and Jelly, Honey
by M Dawn Thacker

I'm spending part of the day with my mother today. She's seventy-five years old and I've only noticed recently that she is one of the elders in my life. I've never thought of her aging until lately. I've worked with elders my whole life, you'd think I'd notice one in my own family, be able to point her out and stamp her with a label. Could I place her on my shelf of favorite wrinkled folks and search for the next one? It may work that way in the nursing home, but not in your own family, not with your own Mama.

Realization sneaks up on you when it's your own flesh and blood. Maybe it's because I know I will be the next generation after she leaves me; my mortality will be showing. Maybe I can't fathom her not being at the other end of the telephone when I need comfort or a recipe; I can't imagine her gone when I reach out to hug her. Maybe it's all of these things, and maybe it's just too hard for me to think about.

She spends most of her time in the kitchen. If she's not baking cakes, she crafting home cooked meals for us: spare ribs, pressure cooked until tender and then broiled brown; scalloped potatoes made with sharp cheddar cheese; green beans from the garden; applesauce made from the Winesaps in her yard; and for dessert, my favorite, egg custard pie.

I called her on the phone.

"What are you up to?" I asked.

"Up to my elbows in jam and jelly, Honey," she said.

She learned the art of canning and preserving from her mother and preserves over one thousand pints of pickles, jams, jellies, relishes, and other colorful condiments in glass jars that I recognize, but cannot always name. Their tastes tickle the tongue. There's no way that her family could possibly eat all of these. Just imagine, every year 1,000 jars filled. If we do the math, that would be 2.7 jars to eat per day. You can't keep this woman from her passion. Try to get her to slow down. She can't throw even one tomato away. After sharing with family, putting aside her Christmas presents, and a secret stash for her doctors, church friends, and reunions, she still has lots left over. These she sells, like today.

We park the car in the field at the farm hosting the Vintage Apple Festival. I look to my right and there she is, the hatch on the back of her van open, table set with the same green tablecloth she always uses, the one from my childhood.

On her table is a profusion of color in glass jars, their insides sparkling and vying for attention. She stands behind the display, collecting five dollar bills for each jar, then wraps each selection lovingly in paper bags. She is also giving out recipes as fast as people ask for them. She is smiling and laughing. She is in her element. She is my mother and no one else's. Mine.

Mama is getting older, I see it in her gray hair, in the way that she rocks back and forth, gaining momentum to get up from a chair, struggling to take lids off of jars with arthritic fingers—and how she gets shorter as my boys grow taller. I see it. I just don't want to believe it. She's my Mama and she's supposed to be here forever.

Read This Please

Volume 1 Edition 5 - Stop, you're scaring me!

October 29, 2010

Welcome to ReadThisPlease.com's Scary Edition. Let's pull up some comfy chairs and curl up in a big blanket. It's Halloween—and that means the writers around here are brewing a few tingly tales. Gather the circle and you can be storyteller tonight. Why venture out into the cold and dark when we can spend an evening together?

Black Angel
by Steven Bird

It's a mile walk from school to the house; the woods
thickening where the pavement ends, at Wheelock Road. The boy
walks alone. He is a shy, introspective boy; the first week at his
new school has been rough. The unexpected and sudden move
from the house on Sylvan Street, having to leave the only home
he'd ever known, his friends and school – everything in his world
seems out of place, drifting. He doesn't like the old house of high
ceilings his parents had rented on the lurch. It's only for awhile,
they said. His father had applied for a new job, out West. The boy
knows that 'out West' is a very long way from Massachusetts,
and that troubles him. Five days to get there, his dad said. He is a
frequenter of woods and brooks, and he'd heard that California is
a desert, and he worried about that, too.

The straight roofline appears, stark, rigid against the clear
autumn sky. The old farmhouse at the end of the road stands
alone, austere and without ornamentation, in the way of its
Yankee builders. The weathered clapboards and shingles remind
the boy of scales, the house, a giant reptile. From the yard, the

window panes look black, the wavy old glass distorting a gray reflection of receding hills, beyond.

The apple tree in the yard is almost bare, the few remaining leaves tattered pennants quivering among a universe of dangling brown orbs. Most of the crop lies on the grass, wormy, misshapen, fallen before the family moved in. As he passes, a crow drops from the branches, rises, and wheels off over the field toward the barren woods.

He lays his books on the dining room table. "Mom, I'm home," he calls. The door to the cellar is open. It's always open. It swings open by itself. That bothers him. He crosses to the doorway and looks down the steps into the musky dark. "Mom?..." Orange light from the furnace isinglass plays over the stone basement walls at the bottom of the stairs. He doesn't like the hollow roar of the furnace. He doesn't like the cellar.

"Hey, I'm in here!" his mother calls from the pantry. She appears in the entry holding a potato. "How'd it go today?"

He looks at his feet. "Alright."

"Made any friends at school yet?"

"I dunno. Maybe. Met a kid who said nobody ever lives in this house very long."

259

Her mouth straightens. She glances to the open cellar door. The hand holding the potato sinks toward her waist a few inches. "Well we won't be living here for long either, not if your father gets the job out West. If that idiot Hawthorne hadn't sold the house out from under us and waited to the last minute to tell us… Don't worry. Won't be long, we're gonna move to California." She smiles.

A dead hornet lays on the step, under the window at the top of the stairwell. The boy bends to pick it up by one stiff wing, avoiding the black abdomen, the stinger at the end still intact. He comes up even with the window and stops on a stair. He places the hornet on the sill beside a row of identical bodies. Seven. That makes seven black angels, the boy notes. He leans into the window and exhales against the pane, watches his breath appear and fade; watches the low sun slant rose light against the chicken house, the uncut field of yellow grass bent almost flat with the seed of a passed season. A line of skeletal maples. Pale sky.

In the hallway leading from the landing, on the expanse of wall between the bedrooms, where, that morning, there had only been the flower print wallpaper, is a picture of Jesus, in the garden at Gesthemane, praying through the night. A beam of light shines down through the olive trees to illuminate His face. The boy stops to examine the picture. Jesus looks sad. In the lower left

260

of the scene, he thinks he discerns a figure not quite formed, a shadow, hidden in the darkness of the rocks and vegetation, leaning toward Jesus, to whisper, maybe.

He is having a hard time getting used to his bedroom. It is a big room with high ceilings. The old armoire seems to crouch, ready to jump and scamper on its clawed feet. It came with the house. His bed and furniture, assembled at one end, don't fill half the room. A straight, ladder-back chair stands solitary by the closet door at the opposite end of the room. He'd hung up the picture of the best battleship he'd ever drawn, but it still didn't feel like his room.

The closet door is open again. He'd closed it that morning. No matter how many times he closed that door, it was open every time he returned to the room. He takes off his school shirt.

His clothes fill only a token amount of space inside the closet. He looks up. The hatchway leading from the closet to the attic is open again, the wooden lid pushed away to expose a square black hole in the white ceiling. Like the cellar door, it opened by itself when nobody was looking. He'd told his mother and father about it. "Just the house shifting. It's an old house." That's what his father said. He pulls the chair into the closet, stands on the seat, and then climbs onto the wooden pole that serves as a hanger rack. His feet shift on the narrow rod clinking

261

the empty hangers seeking balance while his arm fishes up in the dark for the cover.

Gunshots erupt from the saloon. Miss Kitty screams. Marshall Dillon and Chester hustle toward the door drawing their guns. Blue television light plays on his face. The boy admires those men. They were brave. They went toward danger, and saved the day. Miss Kitty screaming reminds him of his mother's scream. It woke him up the night before. "DAVID!" she screamed his father's name, "DAAAVID!" It was in the middle of the night. It woke him up, and then he saw their light under the door. He heard them talking but couldn't make out what they said. His mother sounded worried, his father, concerned. It sounded like they were looking for something. Then his mother hung the Jesus picture up while he was at school…

They've been whispering a lot. His mother and father.

They're in the dining room going over the bills. He catches pieces of their conversation from the living room, his father telling his mother that he is going to put latches on all the doors.

A figure appears next to the couch, blocking the television glow…

"Time for bed, Chief," his father's voice wakes him from a dream… He'd dozed off. "Let's call it a night, okay?"

The stairs creak under his feet. The upstairs hall is a black tunnel. Light from the single clamshell wall sconce is a weak splash on the wall and does not illuminate the hallway. He stops to look at the picture. He can barely make out Jesus. But the whispering figure among the rocks is more discernible now, insinuating itself from the outer dark.

The dark bedroom seems to wait. He imagines the armoire scurrying at the switch of the light, running, its mirror precariously tilted and rattling, flashing crazy signals. He switches the light on. The armoire hunkers against the wall, the open closet door reflecting in its mirror.

The boy does not cross down the room to close the door. He does not want to find the entry to the attic open again. He checks under the bed –

The bare floorboards. A few catkins of dust.

He drops his clothes on the floor, pulls his pajamas from under the pillow. He sits on the side of the bed putting his pajamas on, staring at the varnished closet door. The grain pattern looks like a crocodile head with the mouth open. The open door blocks his view of the inner closet and its contents. Just the house shifting, he recalls his father's words, switching the light off.

The boy falls asleep in the ticking room. He is asleep.

The dormant woods beyond the house stir in the night under a billion stars, a colder air mass moving down from the north. A dog barks.

Something wakes him. The boy opens his eyes to darkness so pure that he cannot see his hands before his face. The air is cold, thick.

A potent obscurity beckons from the dark. It coerces him into the moment. It compels him to raise his head and look toward the foot of the bed.

Somebody is standing there.

A tall, thin shadow, a silhouette, darker than the darkness of the room; the head looks big, like it is wearing an odd hat, or a strange, pointed helmet. Though it is featureless black, the boy is certain the figure is looking at him. It does not move or speak.

He tries to actualize it into something or somebody recognizable…

…His throat constricts. This insane mischief is about him. Is here, to meet him. His heart beats furiously, surging blood roars against his eardrums – he ducks under the covers, pulls the blankets tight over his head, too frightened to call out. He lays that way for a long time, waiting.

Time passes, hysterical, down the sweating, breathing dark.

A vision of brave Marshall Dillon enters his thought stream and fortifies him. He gathers enough courage to make a foray...

Slowly, he lifts the edge of the covers, just enough to survey out to the side of the bed –

The visitor is there. Standing beside the bed, right next to him.

It switched positions. To deliberately terrorize him?... That knowledge overwhelms the boy, and pushes him beyond reason. His bladder lets go and soaks the mattress, but he does not notice. He rolls toward the wall, bed covers his only shield. Tremors wrack his body, his breath exhales in sobs and gasps.

In the waiting silence, the wraith sits down on the edge of the bed. The boy feels the mattress compress under weight, the bedsprings yield a hurt yelp.

It is silent. It sits in the bed with him, exuding a palpable, choking malevolence.

The boy is drowning. His breath leaves his body in the form of a long moan, "oooooooo00Ooh..." His ears register the sound, distant, disassociated and having nothing to do with him.

*

His mother switches the light on.

She rushes to the bed, gathers him in her arms. "It's alright now," she says, "It was only a dream. Just a bad dream. You're okay Baby. You were only dreaming." His mother enfolds him, and the boy's sobs convulse against her, diminish, and finally, cease.

Morose entities dwell at the ragged edges of the world, in the outer dark, the boy's mother determines, able to swing open the doors leading to dark places, the cellar, the attic, but not able to manifest in light.

*

His father bolted the doors shut. The light in the bedrooms, and all the lights of the house were kept on for a week. And the doors stayed shut, and there were no visitors in the night. At the end of the week his mother and father packed the station wagon.

The boy rides the back seat, looking through the rear window, watching the house recede. The roofline blends into the trees then disappears. They'd left most of what they had behind.

They weren't taking any furniture. "What about our furniture? our stuff?" the boy asks.

"Too many old things," his mother says, not looking back, "We'll get new stuff in California."

Sipping
by Sarah Scott

I sit here staring out a rain-streaked window. Lemon water on one side of me, a blueberry bagel on the other. Sipping and nibbling, I pass the first few minutes of this gray sky day. Last night I dreamed about *Vampires in the Lemongrove*, a story I am reading. The ending eluded me as I closed the book and tucked myself into bed. I could not understand its simple premise veiled beneath complex sentence structure and subtlety. In my dream, it all made sense, hanging there upside down; my furry skin filled with longing; my dull, gray fangs quivering in hope for night. How odd to be the villain in your own dream. I wonder what it might mean? Am I like the vampires, sucking life out of everyone and everything around me to preserve my own body, my own world. Could this be? My bagel is gone and the children are rising so I must remove myself from this space and go about my day, but my mind will not be far from here or this dream.

Fear of Death by Trularin

(an excerpt)

"I've isolated it!" he shouted.

Steven pulled the phone away from his ear and said, "Easy."

"I've isolated it my friend...after thirteen years, I finally found it!"

Evan wouldn't say what he had found, but was quite excited that he had found it. Steven asked him what is was that he was so excited about.

"We are going out tonight, to celebrate," Evan said. Again, he failed to tell Steven what was so exciting, but Steven was sure he would find out eventually.

That evening, Evan explained that he had isolated the part of the human DNA that makes the body decline. He explained that were it not for a few sequences in a strand of DNA, people could live far longer. Steven ate a steak and listened. Evan was so excited that he talked excessively. Steven had eaten all of his food when Evan was only starting.

Their conversation went back and forth to the point: Evan said that if he were to remove the aging component of human DNA, any DNA, a body would not age. It would continue on until it was killed off by some other means. Steven suggested rationally, there might be a problem with Evan's idea.

"How's that...?" Evan asked.

"If everyone suddenly stopped dying, the Earth would fill rather quickly," Steven replied.

Evan frowned and had a pensive look on his face.

"So you think my research is inappropriate?" There was a tone to Evan's voice. Steven could hear a hint of disappointment.

"No...no, it is a great idea. But I think there is going to be so much attention moving forward that no one is going to ask if they should go forward." Steven comforted Evan, "It is a great project."

"Thanks."

Evan ate in silence. Steven wasn't sure what to say. When Evan finished, he looked at Steven and blurted it out — he had in fact synthesized an active compound that would remove the aging part of DNA. Steven stopped and stared at his friend. The restaurant went silent, as though they were stuck in time.

"Are you serious?" Steven asked. His eyes glared.

Evan nodded yes. He looked directly at Steven. There was only truth in what Evan had said. Steven lowered his voice and leaned forward.

"You mustn't tell a soul. They will kill you and pervert your discovery. Copy your notes immediately."

Guest of Honor

by B G Lewis

"Bess?"

"Yes."

"Who's Sam—huinn?"

"It isn't really a 'who', Augustine."

"He's dead! That's who he is!" snapped a voice from across the bed.

"Twist! You mind your manners! Shush yourself!" Bess, the oldest, sat straight in the cold loft air and pulled another blanket over herself and her youngest sister. "Don't listen to her, Augustine."

"Twist, do you see Daddy?"

"I can't... you two are talking too much. It's hard to see." Twist sat next to them, covers to her chin, a night bonnet pulled low, over her eyes. Her lips were pursed in concentration.

Beyond a small window, a willow branch reached through the October rain and scratched the glass.

"Bess?"

"Yes, Augustine."

"I miss Polly."

"I miss Polly, too, Augustine."

"Why couldn't Polly stay?"

"She had to go."

"She's happy... isn't she, Bess?"

"She's happy, Augustine."

Suddenly, Twist jolted from the covers and sat upright, her bonnet still over her eyes and down to her nose. "I see him! I see Daddy!"

"Has he got it? Has he got it?" Augustine leaped over Bess to her sister's side, clenching her own eyes to see the image.

Twist continued, "I can't see... wait! He's trudging... in the leaves... he's carrying something... he's got it!"

Augustine could no longer control herself and squealed. Bess, now wide-eyed and quite awake, held Twist's hands. Augustine wrung hers.

"Bess! Augustine! Twist! You three, pipe down! Your father will be home any minute." A mother's reprimand trailed through a fold in a gray curtain, downstairs, and into the lantern's glow over a kitchen hearth.

The girls fell to whispering, full of excitement.

"Can you see? Can you see?"

"No... it's all a bundle," searched Twist.

"Daddy's a wise man. Daddy wouldn't give away the surprise." Augustine glanced to the window and began to compose, "Daddy always picks the best. Daddy always picks the best..."

Twist raised her hand and pressed Augustine's lips. Then she pulled the bonnet from her face and exclaimed, "He's here!"

The girls squealed and scurried under the covers. Three bonnets and three sets of eyes peered out.

Down the steps and into the parlor, a wooden door creaked and then closed with a firm thud. A man's heavy gait crossed beneath the loft and into the kitchen. A deep voice rang clear.

"Here it is, love. Help me with that."

"Oh! It's wonderful! The girls will be thrilled."

If one was to peer up the steps, they might have spied those same eyes now stacked atop each other and sneaking glimpses from the curtain. A giggle gave them away.

"All right, you three. Come down. See what your fine father has brought you."

A tumble of nightgowns and golden locks cascaded over the steps and into the warmth, circling the large, kitchen board, whereupon a young woman was stretched. She was pretty, with long auburn curls, adorned in a modest frock, and quite dead.

"Daddy, she's beautiful!" Augustine fingered tats of lace along the girl's garment. Bess ventured a touch on the girl's bare hand and Twist stroked away damp locks that fell over the open eyes.

The father let off his soggy cloak and smiled, "Well, my dears, I would say your father did a fine job of picking, now didn't he?"

Augustine rushed to his side and embraced him, "Daddy, I knew you would."

The mother lifted the dead girl's limp legs and pulled down the gunny sack.

"She is rather good, dear. Not a blemish. Too good... How did you...?"

"Oh! I seized the opportunity. There was a creek right there. You know, at Ol' Miller's..."

"Aah, I thought you were soaked from the rain."

Twist curled a lock of the girl's hair through her fingers, "Can we help?"

"Of course you can, Twist. Everybody helps this year. Now let's busy ourselves, or your mother will scold." He smiled and winked to his wife, "Where's dinner?"

All three sisters rushed for their father's supper: a large bowl of stew, a heavy loaf, and a flask of cider.

The man settled on the bottom step that led to the loft and regarded his hunger, "Ah darlings, I am famished... Oh! I nearly forgot... Twist... here. This is for you." From his watch pocket, he pulled two bright copper coins, each emblazoned with the head of a ruler. "Hold them, Twist, this year you set the coins."

The young girl clasped the metal in her hands, "Thank you, Daddy."

Mother called her three daughters to task, "Right then, Bess, bring the buckets. Let her arms lie. Twist, you comb the hair. And Augustine, I want you to wash the feet."

All three sisters set about diligently. Bess stepped onto the porch and returned, setting two wooden pails beneath the board. Then she rolled the girl's sleeves up to the elbows and hung each arm into a bucket. Twist claimed a large comb from the mantel and began untangling the long strands. Augustine dipped a cloth in soapy water and washed both of the girl's feet.

When they had completed their duties, Mother pulled a small, sharp blade from her sideboard and took her position on a stool next to an arm. She felt the length of the wrist and made a quick slit. Then she repeated the motion on the other side.

"Bess, you mind the letting. As much as it will... to the last drop."

"Yes, Mother."

"Now, Augustine. Fetch my nice pink and pearl slippers from the bed chest."

"Yes, Mother."

"Twist, my child?"

"Yes, Mother?"

"Fetch my darning needle and some pretty color... let's say, golden thread... like your hair. Quick."

"Yes, Mother."

Augustine returned and fit two ribbon and suede slippers onto the girl's feet. Bess took her position beside her father, who now languished over a pipe and wafted blue trails of smoke into the lantern's glow. Twist held a long needle and skewered the eye with a glimmering thread, then passed it to her mother.

"Ah, perfect. Now my child, bring out your father's coins and place them on the eyes."

"Like this, Mother?"

"Yes, that's it. One up, one down... for coming and going. I don't think the King's grace has beheld a prettier girl."

"Mind your tongue, Mother," said Father as he winked again.

"Is it my turn this year, Mother?"

"Yes, Twist. Like your sister before and Augustine next. I'll do one and you can do the other."

Mother looked on the dead girl's face for a moment, found her start, and began to sew. She slid the needle under the pale skin at the top of the cheek, over the coin, and wove back in, just below the eyebrow. The thread was pulled taut and then returned over the coin and into the cheek again. This stitch was repeated a dozen more times, back and forth, around the socket and under the brow, each pass moving gradually around the coin.

"Now it's your turn, Twist. You'll do well... just as you darn."

Twist felt the skin, and positioned the needle as her mother had. She saw its point press upwards beneath the flesh and popped it through. She wove the stitch over the coin and into the eyebrow, pulled it tight and worked her way round the copper with a dozen more. When she was done, she secured a knot and bit the thread short, tucking it just behind the sovereign.

Then she stood back, arranged the girl's hair around the face, and vowed softly, "I'll be your friend forever."

"Well done, Twist!" Father stooped closer to examine her handiwork and patted his daughter's shoulder. "There's your first! A fine job you did."

"Thank you, Father."

All gathered and surveyed the fashioned girl.

"She's beautiful," Augustine whispered.

"She's more than beautiful," Bess followed.

"What do you think, Twist?"

"She's perfect, Mother."

Bess peeked beneath the board, "The letting's done!"

Mother bent and picked up a bucket, then walked to the porch and set it in the night air. She whistled once and closed the wooden door. In moments, growling and yelping sounded outside.

"The hounds help us and they shall receive our little favors," Mother announced solemnly. "Your father and I will dispatch the rest. You, my lovely girls, are still too young."

Suddenly, Augustine exclaimed, "We must name her!"

"Yes, you must," answered Father. "You, my daughters, must choose the name and I will sit her in the parlor... in a seat for the guest of honor."

Father gently scooped the slender form and raised her under the lantern. He kissed her once above the brow, danced her into the parlor, and positioned her on a soft chair.

"We have the name! We have the name!" squealed Augustine.

"Let's have it, then."

Bess looked to her sister, "Polly was my turn, Twist, you pick."

Twist spoke reverently, addressing her father and then their guest,"We will call her... Margaret,"

"That's a fine name," said Father, smiling. "Margaret it is, then."

Mother returned him a flask, now steeped in dark liquid, "Welcome to our home, Margaret."

"Welcome!" All three sisters chimed.

Tucked within their warm covers, the sisters listened to the rain. Twist wove a strand of auburn hair between her fingers. Bess gazed at moonlight dashing past clouds and through the small window. Augustine's soft breathing meant she was close to sleep. Below in the parlor, Mother and Father spoke in muffled, soothing voices, as they did each night.

"Bess?"

"Yes, Augustine."

"Are you happy we have Margaret for Samhuinn?"

"Yes, Augustine, I'm happy."

"And Bess?"

"Yes."

"She's just like Polly, isn't she?"

"Yes, she's just like Polly."

The Attic

by Margaret-Dawn Thacker

I remember this space from childhood. It was shadowy with questions, exciting in my wonder. It smelled of pine and old times. The wooden beams sweated drops of sap in the summer that hardened into amber beads in winter. I opened trunks and sorted through scalloped bordered black and white photographs of my family, and letters tied in blue ribbons. Their fancy faded script spoke of love and longing, homesickness, missing the taste of pot roast and potato salad, buddies being shot, and cold nights without blankets. The envelopes were white with blue and red stripes. Air Mail was stamped across them. The pages were fragile from their unfolding. The words made me sigh when I read them.

My grandmother's wedding dress, nestled in pink tissue, whispered her innocence under my fingers. I pulled apart the translucent paper and touched the white lace with a curious index finger. Tiny pearl buttons, like treasures from a jewel box were encircled by loops of satin. I imagined this cloud of femininity wrapped around my small, skinny body. The gown transforming me into someone more beautiful than I was.

Sometimes, I unwrapped my mother's china tea set with plates that fit in the palm of my hand. I poured imaginary Earl Gray from a pot with a cracked lid. "It broke," my mother told me, "when my cat, Boots, knocked it over a long time ago." I could see Boots, in all of his black and white finery, come to tea with my mother, the Queen. Boots wore high top white fancy foot ware for the occasion. When the dogs arrived, he was frightened away and spilled the tea, upsetting the party, and my mother.

I sat under the light of the eaves, turning the pages of old picture books illustrated with exotic orange birds and line drawings of old black men. I explored green jungles, swinging from tree to tree on vines. Camels carried me to an oasis with a palm tree and mirror bright water. Princes kissed me awake and dwarfs kept me safe from poisonous apples. Sometimes I fell down rabbit holes and met smiling cats. I got lost in time and adventure until my grandpa came looking for me.

"Mom, where are you?"

"Up here," I call back.

My son's feet make the attic stairs squeak under his weight. I see him emerge from below.

"Wow," he says. "This place is a mess."

"I know," I say.

"Do you remember how much fun I used to have in the attic when I was little?" he asks.

"Yeah, I remember."

Stairway to Heaven

by Adrienne S Moody

(Mature: some coarse language)

Guenter and his sister Anke were new to the Catholic school in the northern prairies. They arrived straight from Germany and at first spoke very little English. It was fall when they arrived, and the wheat that grew tall and waved in the wind behind the small high school was the same golden color as their hair.

Julia thought this as she took a solitary walk at lunch hour, having been shunned by her peers for being different. She couldn't bear lunchtime standing or sitting alone while groups all around her hummed like happy little bees in a hive, so she took to walking in the fields behind the school. She meandered through the yellow wheat fields so deeply that the building disappeared and when she looked up she saw the indigo sky stretch out forever above her head.

She thought of Guenter and the rumors that he was buying souls from anyone who wanted to sell. Fifty dollars was a lot of money and, if one believed the gossip, there were souls to be had. Her brother Maken had told her the very same morning, waiting for the bus, that he figured he'd take Guenter up on it. Maken wanted a new pair of jeans and the new Led Zeppelin IV album. *Stairway to Heaven* was played constantly on the radio—a favorite of his and most of the students at St. Vital Grandin High School.

"He's a sucker, Julia. Fifty bucks? Sure I'll sell mine. Who does he think he is? Satan? Ha!" Maken snorted and French-inhaled his Export A cigarette.

"I heard he makes you sign a contract. That true, Maken?" Julia asked. Her eyes searched the distance for the familiar school bus.

"I'll sign whatever he wants. What a Nazi! That's what he is, Julia. Just a Nazi on the make. I'll be enjoying the money and he can do whatever he likes with the contract. Who does he think he is?"

Well, Julia wasn't so sure. Guenter gave her the creeps. He had yellow hair that fell into his creepy, see-through, blue eyes. His skin was pasty white, just like his sister's. But Anke, she was friendly, at least. Both had accents that made them difficult to understand. Anke was quite beautiful, really, with straight, long hair to her waist—the fashion of that time. Both were tall and reed thin. Guenter stood straight like he had a steel rod up his spine. His head seemed glued to his neck and he never looked left or right—just kept those weird blue eyes staring straight ahead—at nothing, it seemed.

Then this "wanting to buy souls" business. Whispers at lunch told of kids heading off to meet Guenter during breaks, wanting to sign the contract. Word was that he kept a couple hundred dollars on him at all times.

A week later she heard Led Zeppelin on the frontroom hi-fi. Familiar strains of *The Battle of Evermore* drew her from the bedroom to sit next to her brother on the sofa.

"So you did it, huh?" She asked after the song completed.

He just smiled at her and closed his eyes, lost in the band's hypnotic melody and lyrics. Whenever she experienced times alone, she sought out her brother. He allowed it and she always knew when to leave him alone. This was one of those times. The subject was never brought up again and, when he brought home his new Levis, she just commented on how great they looked.

He just smiled.

A month later, it happened. She heard her mother at the back door speaking with alarm to Maken. Julia poked her head around the back door to see him standing in soaking, wet clothes, his hair plastered to his forehead. It was Halloween and she was just dressing-up to go skulking with a new friend she'd made earlier that week. Too old to go trick or treating, they decided to try their luck anyway, dress like gypsies, and maybe bump into some cute guys along the way.

"You what? You fell into the river?" Julia's mother was incredulous, "Maken, that's an unlikely story! You get yourself into the hot tub and into dry clothes. You'll be sick and spread it through the house and I'll get no peace!"

Maken brushed by Julia and she could see he was shaken—to his bones shaken. He was pale and his teeth chattered so loudly Julia thought they might break. She decided to cancel her plans and hang around, in case he might tell her what's going on.

Around midnight she could hear another Led Zeppelin tune, *Going to California.*

*

She followed the melody downstairs stepping gently, not wanting to disturb her brother. He slept in the furnace room—it was the only room that had a door that he could lock. He and his girlfriend, Lee, liked to hide in there after school to neck, and he'd hook the doorknob up with an electrical current to keep his siblings out.

The door was open.

Inside was dark, but she could make out his form on the bed.

"Maken?" she whispered after the song completed.

No answer.

"Maken, are you okay?"

"Yeah.."

"Can we talk?"

No answer, so she took it as a "yes."

She stood at the doorway and could make out his face now, set and solemn.

"What happened tonight? You can talk to me."

"Jesus, Julia, I can't believe what happened."

"Tell me. I'm not going to tell anyone."

"You know Louis Cardinal?"

"Oh yeah," she did know him. Everyone did. He was an angry, scary guy.

"He held a knife to Jeff's throat a month ago—and made him suck him off. Afterward, he told Jeff that if he told anyone, he'd slit his throat. So tonight I ran into him—walking home from school. I freaked, Julia. I tore off and he chased me. Man, I ran— across the trestle, the only way to go, and he kept after me, and then a train came the other way—I could hear it—and you know how you can hear the vibration of the tracks when it gets close?"

Julia nodded and sank into the mattress at the foot of his bed.

"I knew I'd never make it, Julia. I could see it rounding the corner, so I fucking jumped."

"Oh no!"

"Oh yes! I thought I was dead at first, you know?" She nodded. "So I swam to shore and I dunno what happened to the asshole. I just wanted out of the water and get my sorry ass home. So that's it."

"Are you hurt, Maken?"

"No—not hurt."

"Are you scared?"

Silence, and then, "I think all this is coming down since that Nazi bought my soul. I think I'm cursed, Julia. I'm gonna buy it back."

"Can you? Will he let you?"

"Oh yeah, he will. It's gonna cost me though."

"Really? How much?"

"You can buy it back for a hundred."

"Jesus, Maken."

"Yeah, I know. I'm the sucker. But I don't think my life is worth a cent without it."

Julia sat with her brother while he played the album over from the beginning.

He let her stay and the music played, *Stairway to Heaven.*

The Ferryman
by Adrienne S Moody

Daniel loved Margarette as much as he was capable of loving anyone. She was the mother of his three boys and he chose her specifically for that reason: genetics. He was a short man, standing only 5'6", and as most old school Germans are, demanded the best in everything. He had to fight for everything he acquired in life, even Margarette. He chased her down relentlessly.

"Oh, yes he did," Margarette relayed to their sons' girlfriends and wives. "Daniel wouldn't take no for an answer. And I told him no many, many times. I told him he's way too short for me. And told him he wouldn't do because, well, for one, how would we look on the dance floor? I am 5'11" in my flats!"

"Yes, she did say that," Daniel would add, "and I told her back, how often in our lifetime together are we going to be on the dance floor?"

"And then I told him I would not live an artist's life. I grew up in that environment. All the partying, drinking and such that

went on in my household growing up! No, not for me. I told him
no."

"And I kept at her and I wore her down."

"How did you wear her down, Daniel?" Lauren, the eldest
son's fiance asked.

"He LIED to me! He said he would give up being a painter
for a real job. He would paint only as a hobby."

"I was too good. What choice did I have?" Daniel raised his
hands, palms up and shrugged his shoulders to accentuate his
point. "You have to admit, I supported our family very well on
my income as an artist."

"Yes, you did. But, Daniel..." her voice trailed off and she
cast her eyes down in sadness.

She did not have to say anymore. Daniel loved the single
women who were like stray cats poised and sprawled at his feet at
their many parties. It took little effort for him to bed down any of
the young adoring creatures. Such a waif knocked one evening,
during dinner. He opened the back door to Mimi, his conquest the
night before, looking at him, hopelessly obsessed. He told her to
go on home, that he was a married man with no future plans for

her. He opened the door wider, so she could see his family seated, forks raised midway to their mouths, their eyes wide in disbelief.

This is the life he offered Margarette and because of the children, she tried to make it all work. She tried to join in and take on lovers as well. It wasn't what she wanted; it was what she had.

After retirement and the boys set out on their own, the couple moved to a remote Island in the Pacific Northwest, inhabited by writers, potters and artists like himself. There was one cafe that served the Islanders hot coffee, bacon and eggs, soups, sandwiches, and worked double duty as the post office, liquor store, and video rental. Every summer, the inhabitants had a wine competition at the small community center. Blackberries were the berries of choice and this made for the event of the year.

Their life settled to quiet normalcy for the first time in their strained married life. Margarette had the largest and most productive garden on the Island. Daniel had to build her a seven foot high, wire fence around the vegetables to keep out the deer.

Life was good, until Margarette was diagnosed with bone cancer. At first, they thought it was a problem a chiropractor could fix. Months went by with no relief and she was finally advised to go for a bone scan. For the first time in their marriage,

295

Daniel needed to be there for Margarette and care for her. And that he did.

Cocktails of drugs were mixed in the kitchen at all hours of the day and night. Morphine and morphine accelerators were used to try and keep the pain tolerable. She refused to go into the hospital and be drugged into a coma which is what she heard they eventually do. She wanted to see life as vividly as she was capable as long as she could.

Their boys came to visit often. She became attached to Yvette, a French girl her youngest boy Andy had taken up. Yvette brought videos for them to watch and one such video was about angels. It was a documentary about people who were saved by angels. Story after story depicted how human beings were detoured off death's road by these heavenly creatures. It affected Margarette.

"Maybe I ought to reconsider getting help with this," she whispered to Yvette in the TV room after the film ended.

"What do you mean, Margarette? Help with what?"

"Our doctor is very compassionate. She has given us what we need to make my pain... shorter. Assisted suicide, to be technical. We're reading a book about it. Every morning I ask Daniel, 'If today is a good day?' and if he feels ready to do this for me. He will say yes. If he cannot bear it, he will decline. We started last week."

"You are ready to go, Margarette?" Yvette asked tearfully and held onto a hand that felt like a broken sparrow.

"The pain is so bad. Some days I think I'll go mad. I am ready. But what if, like the movie showed, I can be saved at the last minute? Maybe this is wrong..."

Yvette did not have the answer, so did not speak. They sat in silence, listening to the sounds of the surf outside. The following morning, Yvette and Andy left on the ferry and life on the Island became a day-by-day evaluation of whether life should be lived.

On a dreary, late October morning, Daniel answered yes to his wife's question.

He stood in the kitchen with shaking hands. In his mind, he did the deed hundreds of times. He did not anticipate this cold fear in his gut. He mixed the deadly concoction and filled the syringe. The sun was just rising; it was 6:20 AM. He saw a man walking in front of his property, stepping heavily on the oyster beds. He shouldn't be there as it was private property. In the ten years that they lived there, no one ever trespassed. Not at this hour.

To his disbelief, he saw the dark figure turn to their cottage and walk toward the door. Daniel quickly scooped all the bottles, the syringe, and placed them in the drawer by the sink.

Daniel waited.

A knock made the blood pulse loudly in his ears. He felt ill, but knew he had to answer the door, so he opened it.

"Yes?" he spoke to a tall, thin man wearing a trench coat, jeans and running shoes. He had a long distinguished nose and narrow lips. His eyes looked moist and the warmest brown.

"I am new to the Island and thought I'd drop by and say hello," the stranger spoke.

"This is not a good time. My wife is not well, you see."

"Oh, I am so sorry to hear that. Sick is she?"

"This is not a good time. Some other time. Maybe," Daniel closed the door slowly, but purposefully. He locked the deadbolt, pressed his ear to the door and listened. He felt he could hear the stranger breathing on the other side. He waited.

"Daniel..." Margarette called out to him weakly.

"Yes, yes I am coming."

Daniel went to the drawer and retrieved the syringe which was loaded and glanced out the window. The stranger stood at the shoreline facing his cabin.

Watching.

It was easier than he thought. After the injection, while her eyes were still open, and she was there with him, he held her hand.

"Are you angry with me, Margarette? Are you angry that I lied to you?" he whispered, tears dropping on the bed sheets.

She didn't answer, just looked deeply into his eyes and slowly drifted away.

He called his sons later that afternoon and told them that their mother was gone and that she went peacefully. Only Yvette and Andy knew the truth.

"The strangest thing happened, Andy. Someone showed up at the door around 6 AM. The oddest thing—him walking the beach in front of our place. He actually came up to the door and wanted to visit. Can you imagine? At 6 AM? I told him my wife was sick and told him another time. Closed the door before he could say anything more."

"That is strange, Dad."

"Very strange, Daniel," Yvette concurred, listening on the extension.

"I took it as a sign, actually. I took it as a sign that I was doing the right thing."

Andy agreed and supported his Dad, telling him that he did her a favor, and it was courageous for him to put his loving wife to rest without anymore agony.

Yvette said nothing.

Prota Caprine

by B G Lewis

Never mind the seas you sail, a change will come, some header or lift and without warning. Those that find the edge will make fair time. Others hitch a lull and sit for days. Or worse, find the rocks.

In time, you can be wondering on some far off place while the whole of nature and machine will settle in the wind together. It's a spell and the finest of sailors cannot tell you how it occurs, or account for their hand on the wheel. The sense comes from salt in the blood and distance in their eyes.

Landon Crowel had that look. He was a tiring son of a bitch and he'd run 40 men and 80 tons from Maine to the Keys more times than most live in years. He'd killed as many souls, and half with his bare hands, but he'd never lost a ship.

A day's leg out of Portsmouth, he sent a sharp-mouthed bastard with no years up the spar and the lad dropped into a bowline. His neck snapped clean and the body was sent to the water. The old Crow never lifted an eye. He felt the weight leave

301

the ship. That devil would only call to the men, "Leave the head. It'll gather the gulls and we might be needin' to eat them."

I have seen reasonable men turn sour under hard captains, but none as hard as the master of the Prota Caprine. If the siren Lilith herself could spawn a brother for Lucifer, he'd not match the cruelty of Landon Crowel.

So it was, when war spread from the land's end to the sea, came the Caprine flying color under the hammer of Crowel and full sail into the thick of death. It was on that ship I learned to hate a man, and not a simple despising. I yearned for his throat within my hands, to watch his eyes and wring life from this earth, ridding us all of a terrible thing.

*

As the ship's luck increased, dark whispers spread among the crew: a secret was kept by Crowel and shared with none, not even his bosun. There was reason he carried no fear into battle. Somewhere in the dank holds of the Caprine there was said to be a cargo, and not lade by human hands. Landon Crowel had claimed himself a talisman, a charm, and hid it away from all eyes.

In the recounting of these matters, I will not diminish my virtue by admitting that I know the nature of Crowel's ways.

What men do to remain alive is their affair. Yet in hope's stead, sailors will keep curious traditions. It may be the haunting of the waves or the wind's moan in the topmast, whatever the cause, there are visions and dreams that fill the mind after a length at sea, and the crew aboard the Prota Caprine were no different.

A fortnight from our last shore, I ventured on deck to see the comforting glow of Orion for myself. The weather had broke and we were running trim day and night. The watch, wary he be kicked in the shins for napping—or worse, caught by the Crow— hung a noose over his own head to keep steady on the wheel. I gave no notice and kept myself unseen, keeping astern to chance a chew of tobacco. There I spied a glimpse of Crowel's evil ways. I saw that thing that lurked the days in the belly of the ship.

There, with raven locks flown in the wind, was a figure at the foredeck and standing on the rail. Its cloaked shape rocked and balanced oblivious to the waves below. This dark wraith was smelling the spray and pawing at the sky. I fell among the coiled halyards lest it see me and claim my life then and there. To name this beast of darkness, I cannot. Yet when this thing turned and lay its gaze upon me, I knew then, that I would soon be responsible for unmentionable deeds.

*

Twelve days in a hold.

I've not ate nor drank, but what she feeds me, and she feeds me not. I want to run and flee, but she holds me, singing and taunting. I am terrified of her—I am her slave, yet I wear no chain.

I remember begging to remain in full composure, awake. I plead that I might leave, a secrecy, and our interlude but chance. Still she lulled me, and I drifted. Such would be my demise, for when I awoke in her presence, the soles of my feet were gone—down to the bone. I struggled to crawl, but the pain—I was wrought. She soothed me and I returned to dream.

When I awoke at the second instance, my flesh had been removed from my feet and ankles. I witnessed my own bare, raw, bones and was mortified. I screamed until a palsy overcame me and I have since wandered only close to consciousness, cursing my ill choice to board this ship and serve the henchman Crowel. The planks of the cursed frigate have now faded, though I writhe within its cavern.

A mesmerizing vision oft greets me and I only recall occurrences with vagary. The skin of my hands has fallen away, leaving knuckle without sinew or fiber, not a portion of what nature had given me, but for bare, wet, bone.

Waking is now a phantasm. She comes to my side from shadow and examines my wounds fervently. So intent she is, that she never speaks, only sings, and wanders in tone and phrase. She spreads a tincture upon approach and I slip in thought, returning to myriad.

I know the twelfth day passes, as she has told me. In my wavering mind, she comes to me and all my wants are to lie at her feet, panting. I am an animal she beckons.

The flesh is now gone from my appendages. I feel my skull is bare. With great effort, I focus my vision upon my exposed carriage and the rib work gleams. I am an atrocity. I am doomed.

She has done this act upon me and it is by her hand and breath that I am now ruin, the visage of death, a frame of what was. Yet, she comes to feed again. Her face rests within my belly and she sups upon my bowels. Her gnaw rattles my spine. I will rest once more and then she will consume my countenance and kiss me a last time.

*

On this, the last and thirteenth day, I wake beside her, but I cannot feel her. She is beautiful, but I cannot see her. She sings to me sweetly, and I long to hear her ancient melody. I long to hear the sea again.

"Prota Caprine, Prota Caprine," she spreads flowers through my mind, "Come to me, Prota Caprine, tonight we ride again!"

Hallways

by Bruce Reisner

temptation to trespass
maids steal change off of nightstands
all this happened on an end table
I walked through glass double doors
on impulse
wanting nothing
not even to steal some cherries
though each kitchen had bowls of them
and peaches and figs
with nobody there to object
my back to the walls none the less
I flat-footed out of each apartment
hallways kept telling me bullshit
finding the glowing exit
I exited back into hallways
and back into stainless steel kitchens
and back into cinder block halls
each exit taunted
the sleeping trespassing hiker

The Saltchuck
by Sheila Cano

In the moments before waking, Kenna looked into dark water and saw a face just under the surface. As sleep ebbed away, Kenna felt certain this was not a dream, but a message. Was it a woman or a man? She would check for news when she went into town.

The pearl grey morning reflected in the water. Low swells defined the difference between sea and sky. Closer to shore, an oily saltchuck, the channel where fresh water draining down a stream from Lake Morgan mixed with the ocean tides of the bay, concealed many things: rocks that could strand a boat, seaweed that coils around a swimmer's legs, stinging tentacles of jellyfish, and rotting debris. A black cormorant flew in a straight line two feet above the water, heading for the guano-splattered islet where seals bask. A gull's cry over the slapping waves played rhythm and counterpoint to Kenna's mood as she walked to the general store.

"How's it goin', kiddo?" Marge said, peering through smeared bifocals and handing Kenna the mail over the counter.

Kenna glanced around the store, knowing her every gesture was being examined by the regulars. The favourite entertainment of locals was watching neighbours and dissecting personalities.

"Oh, fine, and you?"

"Not too bad, thanks." You haven't run into our Terry Calder yet today, have you? I guess he's not back. Last I heard, he took his boat out around Black Rocks."

Did I dream it? Maybe this is real...

Kenna felt a hot stream of anxiety pool with images she had envisioned earlier. She knew Terry from around town. He was friendly enough. A handsome young man with cheerful eyes. If she was ten years younger she'd consider flirting with him, but he was busy and always on the go. He helped support his aging father with a small fishing trawler. Terry would be a catch for one of the local girls.

"That doesn't sound good. I hope he's all right," Kenna offered.

"Troubles the mind. Best we not spread stories, right?"

"He'll show up."

"You just keep an eye out if you're on the beach walkin', dearie," Marge said as she regarded Kenna solemnly over the bridge of her spectacles.

Kenna grimaced at the thought of finding a corpse bobbing in the water. She walked back to her cottage. Halfway, she noticed a pattern in the fir needles scattered on the forest path. They appeared to be arranged. It reminded her of ancient stone carvings or cave paintings. Images of people, animals and plants were twined together, shifting and changing. It's just nature playing games, Kenna told herself. When she looked up, in the distance a figure came gliding toward her, moving without walking.

"Terry! What are you doing here? Are you all right? We thought you drowned."

Terry Calder stood before Kenna. He seemed to cry out, but she heard nothing. His face was gripped in anguish. He looked frantic, unsure of himself. Kenna's scalp tingled. She closed her eyes and then opened them quickly. Terry had vanished. She stumbled forward, not feeling the path beneath her feet. The last hundred yards home felt like a dream.

At the cottage, Kenna closed the door behind her and bolted it. She put on the kettle for tea. The familiar task occupied her hands, while she replayed the morning in her mind.

Life on the coast: starting fresh had been her plan, but it hadn't brought her any peace. While camping last summer, she suddenly remembered Gene, a family friend. She hadn't thought about him for forty years. She tried to recall his last name, going letter by letter through the alphabet, hoping one would trigger her memory. She pictured him, his family, their house, anything to bring his name into her mind. When she arrived home, she called her father to let him know she was safe.

"Hi, Pa. I'm back from the wilds. How are you?"

"Hi, Babe. I'm good - but I have some sad news. Gene Gardner died last week."

"Oh, no. I'm sorry to hear that. This is crazy - I've been thinking about him for two weeks. I couldn't remember his last name."

"Well, you must have been only ten years old, the last time you saw him."

"How did he die?"

"An embolism. No warning."

Kenna felt a wave of apprehension push against her. The kettle boiled over. Steam scolded and hissed, returning her to the present.

I should be used to this, but I'm not. If this is a gift, I don't want it. It doesn't do anybody any good - I can't stop anything.

"So what's your take on the new gal?" Old Johnny said as he took off his trucker cap and whacked it against his jeans.

"I don't know. Haven't figured her out yet. Kinda hard to know what she's thinkin'."

"City folks are like that. 'Fraid they'll give somethin' away. But they open up some after bein' here awhile."

"Any news about Terry? I seen the boys tow his boat over. The engine's dead."

"This is all pretty hard on Jack, Marge, don't be talkin'. That kid's all he's got."

Marge and Old Johnny sat facing the inlet, watching the fishboats ply their way into dock one by one.

The tea calmed Kenna's nerves and she finished a second cup. She picked up her flashlight, sweater and toque, unbolted the door and headed down to the shore to look for Terry. The tide was coming in. If her dream was true, he could have been in the water for several hours. She took the long way, using the wooden steps instead of the forest trail. She needed to be steady and solid, not subject to the whims of her imagination.

Picking her way out over the slimy cobblestones, Kenna slipped more than once. Memories and past premonitions crowded her mind. Twenty years ago, at work one day, she called her mother but got no answer. She called again later, same thing. Leaving the office, she drove to her mother's apartment instead of going home. When her knocking received no reply, she let herself in. Her mother lay on the floor, cold and no longer alive.

The memory brought tears and blurred her vision. Kenna stopped and sat on a log, rested her elbows on her knees and held her head in her hands. She wept. Twenty years ago, and she still felt the anguish, the shock and the solitude of finding her mother's body.

Oh, Mom, I'm so sorry. I'm sorry that you suffered so much. I love you, Mom.

313

A kingfisher's rattling call startled Kenna. She wiped her eyes with her sweater, stood up and headed for the tide line. It would do no one good to dawdle now; the light would soon fade.

If I could find Terry's body, at least his father would know what happened to him, at least Terry would be back home.

She walked along the water's edge, checking each tide pool and broken rock big enough to catch whatever might wash ashore. From a distance, a big piece of seaweed-covered driftwood resembled someone lying on the beach. Kenna shook her head to dislodge the image. Rounding the point, she climbed the low dune overlooking the bay. Here the water was deeper, dark green and murky. She strained to see beyond the surface reflections, alert to any movement, any odd shape. Gulls lofted overhead, holding position as if stopped in time.

Kenna saw a pale limb attached to a rounded head.

Oh, God, there he is. That must be him.

She exhaled, watching an octopus disappear behind the rocks.

"Jeez, Kenna," she said to herself.

Looking across the bay, the opposite shore was no longer visible. It had become too dark and the weak sunlight was swallowed by a band of thick sea-mist creeping towards her. She would have to put off her search until morning.

The villagers listened to the radio news that evening, each one grateful to be home, dry and warm.

"I seen that girl Kenna down by the point," Marge said to her friend Gail. "She was starin' into the bay, lookin' real hard."

"Probably looking for some sign, don't you think? We're all looking. Besides, she's not a girl, she's a grown woman," Gail replied.

"Funny, she don't seem all that grown up to me. Seems like a girl, still. City people just don't know what real life is 'til they come out here." Marge cleared the dinner dishes and wiped down the plastic tablecloth.

"Yeah, well, she's finding out now, isn't she? I just feel so bad for Terry, wish there was something we could do."

Kenna switched on her flashlight as she entered the forest. It was quicker going home this way, even though she felt apprehensive about what might lurk in the bushes. She felt a rush of warm air behind her, then tripped on a cedar root, falling forward. The flashlight rolled a few feet away, stopped, and blinked, then died. She pushed herself to her feet and turned around. The sound of rasping breath came from the trail, but she could see nothing. The black outline of the trees stood in silhouette against a coal grey sky.

Then...

"You have come to the right place."

"Who's there? Who are you? I can't see you," Kenna crouched, squinting into the night.

"Do not be afraid. Just watch your step - don't slip. Here's your flashlight."

The beam glowed suddenly, thrust toward her by an invisible hand. She snatched the flashlight and turned it in the direction of the voice. But it showed only tall firs while the path and the underbrush were revealed.

I must be going mad. This can't be happening. This can't be real.

"Where are you? Who am I talking to?"

"Yourself. You're talking to yourself."

Kenna screamed. A long wail forced its way out of her lungs. Shining the flashlight ahead, she ran toward home. Her legs ached and she staggered, trying not to fall again. Rushing to the opening at the edge of the forest, she saw a dim light glowing from outside her cottage. She didn't remember turning the porch light on before she left.

"Did ya hear that?" Marge looked at Gail, eyebrows raised.

"Sounded like a banshee."

"I think it come from that Kenna's place. Better go see, c'mon."

Marge pulled on her wool jacket and grabbed the lantern, with Gail close behind her. They jogged the hundred yards along the gravel path, arriving at the doorstep moments before Kenna ran up, panting hard.

"Hey, kiddo, are ya okay? We heerd this awful yell."

Marge grasped Kenna's arm, pulling her onto the porch.

"Oh, thank God it's you. I've just had a scare, coming through the forest."

She hugged Marge tightly and reached out to grasp Gail's hand. But Kenna didn't want to confide that she was talking to a mysterious voice along the path. Her friendship with Marge and Gail was too delicate at this point.

"Well, you're out wanderin' at night in this fog, no wonder yer upset. You should make a cuppa tea, that'll fix ya."

"I think a stiff drink might be better," Kenna said. "Please have one with me, will you?"

"Naw, thanks, we gave 'er up some time back," Marge said. "Had one too many, years ago, dearie. If ya feel OK, we'd best be gettin' home."

"I really appreciate your coming by."

Kenna went inside, turned on the reading lamp and closed the door. Then she walked to the pantry and poured a small shot of whiskey into a teacup. She gazed into the amber liquid briefly, then downed it. As the alcohol burned her throat and its warmth spread through her body, she eased into her chair and fell asleep.

Kenna woke with a sore neck. She rubbed the muscles on her shoulder through breakfast, anxious to get back out to the beach. The sun poked through the low cloud cover, dappling the sea in patches of blue and green. Kenna resumed her patrol along the shoreline, walking all the way to the cove beyond the bay. The Coast Guard boat passed half a mile out, followed by a Zodiac. She stopped and sat on a large boulder above the water.

Maybe they will find him. I'd rather they did. They must have looked everywhere by now.

A clump of kelp drifted in the water, sloshed against a boulder and washed back as the current sucked it away. Kenna saw the pale glow of facial features a few feet under. She studied the shape and it blended with her own reflection. The features were paler than her own, and the hair was shorter and unkempt. She closed her eyes and opened them again. The face was still there. She turned away and took a few steps, then vomited her breakfast onto the sand.

Kenna resolved to secure the body. If she ran back to the village, the corpse might slip under the kelp or get caught by the current and wash into the bay. She stumbled over the sea moss to where she could stretch an arm and grab the shape floating just beneath the surface. Her fingers fluttered in the water. A few more inches...then Kenna slipped. She twisted into the froth and went under. Her back hit a jagged rock that knocked the breath from her. She gasped and her lungs filled with brine. Panic took over and she screamed in bubbles. Her legs thrashed but wouldn't turn her body. Seaweed enveloped her, winding over her arms and head. Reflections swirled above; the light dimmed and she sank deeper. Kenna looked through the dark water to the surface and saw a pale face. It was Terry, looking intently at her. He was calling, but she heard nothing.

His face is gripped in anguish; he looks frantic, unsure of himself.

Kenna felt herself drift into unconsciousness; she felt certain this was not a dream.

"Gail, Marge, you two better sit down." It was Old Johnny, gesturing toward the bench outside on the boardwalk.

"You look pale, Johnny." Gail studied her old friend carefully.

"It's that girl, Kenna. They finally found the body. She was out at Black Rocks tangled in kelp."

"I knew we should have never left her alone that night," Gail broke down. "She asked us in for a drink. We just made excuses."

"We left when we shoulda stayed." Marge daubed her eyes. "She was actin' so strange, out there starin' at the bay like she knew Terry was - God knows I shoulda bin more thoughtful of her situation, all lonely out there in that cottage with no one but the gulls and the waves."

"Well, it was Terry who found her," said Old Johnny, "but seconds too late. He got his engine goin' and took a run up the saltchuck where the tide brings logs on shore."

Gail clasped her Marge's hand.

"We can't blame ourselves, Marge. None of us can. We're just simple folk. We don't understand those city people's problems."

"Well, she's gone home now," Old Johnny said, looking out to the bay. "She's home now.

I Shivered
by Sarah Scott

I noticed it yesterday, the first signs of the changing season. As I shook the rug out on the back porch, a swarm of butterflies danced about the puffy pink lantana. When the lantana first sprouted this spring it was only a foot or so high, now it reached the tops of windows and almost blocked the sidewalk. Monarch, bright yellow, and semi-transparent butterflies flitted to and fro among the overgrown plant, alighting on a pink bud here, an orange one there. I smiled. Here the leaves don't change until after Halloween, so we look to the butterflies and cicadas for signs. A crisp bite was in the air yesterday as I headed off to class and something about it smelled different, a little like death. I shivered and ran back in for a jacket.

Midnight Dream
by Gaboo

Where do the trees end? Over here. Where do they end? Over here. I was never here before.

Over the hill, look, there's a bear! Go down the hill. I won't. Go down the hill. I won't. Pine tree to hold. Up the hill. A long pine that weaves. Red black bark on the weaving pine. We should have gone up the hill. Climb rocks. Stretch and climb the rocks. We should have gone up the hill. There's a bear back there. Rocks and shale. Slippery, step, step, rocks and shale. Red black bark weaves up the hill. Sun behind the hill. I can see the view. Sun behind the hill. Such a view. Red sky behind the hill.

I live there. Go inside. I live there. Behind the pillars, behind the old door. Go inside. Go behind the pillars behind the red door. Hollow room. Rooms and rooms. Open the door. Hollow room. Old antiques. Someone lived here. I've come to shop. Someone else lived here and I'm shopping on the balcony, because the hollow room isn't there. City below. City below with river piers. Green moss river piers. Lean forward. Over. Stop. Lean forward. Stop. Lean. Let go— over and over. Oh! I can do that again.

Dizzy. I can do that again. So high. Spin. I can do that again. It doesn't mean anything. Spinning doesn't mean anything. Spinning doesn't mean anything anymore...

But she's in a window. She's in a green dress. In the window, in a green dress. The whisper comes. Shiver. Oh, the whisper. I'm near her, but I can't touch. She's in a green dress and I can't touch. She's beautiful. Lights flashing and too many people. Too many people to hear. She lives in the hollow room! I've known her a long time, but she was living in the hollow room. Hair billow, falling, shimmering. She smiles and whispers come. Look! She's beautiful, but I can't hear. Too many noisy people. But I don't know where I knew her—? Where did we meet? She knew me and I'm missing her. Where's the whisper? Lights flashing and there's too many people. Noisy, they are nothing. Oh, I miss you. This is all noisy and nothing. Where's the whisper? And the people fade.

There's no road. I'm just slowing. Look! That was a town I knew, but I've never been here. I know the people. We should stop because the road doesn't end here. This is a nice town. I've been here but I don't know this place. Fancy little houses, tucked in and trim. This is a nice town. They might have fields. All different town people. Moving and walking. They're not normal—they're not talking. They do the same thing over and

over. I know this town. Robots. This town doesn't have a door
and my ride is gone. Where's the town's door? My ride is gone.
We shouldn't have stopped because the road doesn't end here. See
it over the fields. Stretching fields, far, I want to look. I miss the
green fields. Rolling over and over in mist. Beautiful, trim, rolling
green. Shades of green, billowing grass, wisps of grass,
shimmering. She lives here. I know she lives here. I want to show
you! Come quick! Hurry, she lives here. Please hurry.

She talks in whisper. She smiles and the whisper comes.
Whisper through the dark. Look around the dark. Go around.
Look around the dark, past the dark. Where do the trees end?
Over here. I was never here before.

Personal Curses

by Bruce Reisner

In awe of those possessed of beauty

and selective

I take the elevator down

coax the whip

and let swear words slip

rating each jaw that passes

it should be strong

like an ass's

the nose must not be a bother

can't have been fixed

must be distinguished from the others

the neck firm as black strap molasses

hair of an Aryan lass's

the hat on the bed beside me

and the black cat that denies me

the ladder under which I walk

is able to talk

to this hurtful obsession with beauty

Truth Hurts

by Margaret-Dawn Thacker

One day, a farmer climbed aboard his tractor and tilled the soil. He walked the garden, picking up rocks and throwing dried bits of last year's crop over the fence. When he turned from the barbed wire, he noticed an odd sight. What had been forgotten, something left behind and ignored, suddenly interested the farmer. He bent down and dropped to one knee next to a pumpkin.

"Oh my gosh," the farmer exclaimed, "Where did you come from?"

He reached out and touched Jack's skin, then picked him up and looked where the pumpkin had lain in the straw. The farmer tested the stem and followed Jack's vine to the roots near the edge of the garage.

The farmer scratched his head and said, "Well I'll be dogged, you lived through the winter. You're one strong pumpkin."

The man hurried away and in a few minutes he came back with his wife puffing behind and trying to keep up.

"Can you believe this?" the farmer asked.

"I've never seen anything like it," she said, bending over the pumpkin. "We've had a few volunteer tomato vines and flowers come up, but those grew from last year's seeds. I've never seen a pumpkin plant live through the winter."

She patted Jack and said, "You are one special pumpkin, aren't you Jack?" That's when Jack got his name.

Other pumpkins grew in the patch, but Jack was different. Now he was the oldest, biggest, and wisest of the pumpkins. He'd earned the distinction; he was a tough, hardened, second-year inhabitant of the patch. And, he was the farmer's darling. When the farmer walked through the garden with other people, he stopped at Jack, pointed to him, or patted him, and said, "See Jack here? He's special. I've never had a pumpkin like him. He's destined for greatness." Even when the farmer was alone, he'd make his way over to Jack, rub him, check him for pests, and say, "How are you today, buddy?" Jack shined a little brighter orange as he basked in the attention.

However, life for Jack had not been without struggle. The previous year, Jack had been a late bloomer. When everyone else was harvested, Jack was only the size of a baseball, round, and green. Somehow, his seed sprouted and his vine grew right along the garage wall, under the overhang, and out to the southern end of the garden. Jack was a baby when the rest of the pumpkins were cut from their vines, loaded into wheelbarrows, and set in the wagon behind the garden tractor.

Jack had felt sad and unloved, left behind and alone. When the soil was turned, the plow came within six inches of ripping his roots from the ground. Jack watched and waited, holding his breath, shaking and feeling his insides tangle, until the farmer parked the tractor in the garage for the season.

Jack was relieved that he'd been spared. At the time, it was lonely in the patch with no one to talk to, but a solitary life certainly beat death. This he believed, until the weather changed and temperatures dropped. He had felt frost on his skin once in a while, but not every night. When the cold really set in, Jack sometimes wished he'd been turned over with the dirt and left to rot. At least he would have a blanket of soil over his cold, decomposing body. Jack's vine lost most of its color and became brittle. The smallest leaves froze and dropped to the ground. The edges of the bigger leaves curled and dried. The pace of the garden slowed and its breath became shallow.

Living in the south saved him from a deep freeze, but Jack was hungry most of the time. He felt life slipping a little more each day. The sun that warmed him came up late and set early. Nights were the worst, especially clear nights, when the stars were like sharp bits of ice that penetrated Jack to his core.

The farmer spent a good deal of time in and around the garage. That's what saved Jack. The garage was heated by a wood stove. Jack watched the man take the chainsaw into the forest beyond the garden. He heard the whine and the crack of timber splintering. The man returned, carrying wood and stacked it near Jack's vine. Each day, the farmer came out to the stack, gathered an armload and walked back into the building. After that, Jack heard the crack and pop of fire and felt a slight change in temperature, warming the soil around him. He came to love the sound of the saw, the smell of sap from pine shavings, and the sight of the farmer gathering wood. All of this meant heat.

Jack's growth slowed through Thanksgiving and stopped by Christmas. When he didn't think he could stand the cold one more minute, the days began getting a little longer and warmer. A subtle change came over the garden. It breathed a little deeper and sighed under the sun.

Activity picked up. The farmer turned rows for peas and potatoes, planted hills with squash seeds, ran wire for the beans and cucumbers, and planted more seeds around Jack in the pumpkin patch. They sprouted and bloomed. Bees buzzed and pollinated the flowers. Small pumpkins began growing into baseball-size spheres, just like Jack had grown the year before. Jack welcomed each one as it came to life. He was already orange by this time, and about the size of a honeydew melon.

The smaller pumpkins looked up to Jack, respected his wisdom, and asked him questions about the garden and the farmer. They asked about birds and bugs, and about their purpose in the patch.

"You are pumpkins," Jack told his patch mates with a deep voice of authority. "You will grow to be orange, round and big—not as big as me—but big. The farmer will nurture and water you, keep the bugs from biting you, and dust powdery mildew off your vine. He will bring his family, children, and grandchildren to admire you."

Jack was a storyteller. The farmer's family had talked as they worked the garden and harvested vegetables the year before. Jack listened and now he had tales to tell. He sharpened his skill in the winter when he shivered under the dark, night sky. His imagination became a comfort from the chill. His storytelling grew bolder as he grew bigger and rounder. Jack was quiet during the day, basking in the sun, keeping his thoughts to himself, but at night, he entertained the others. The pumpkins' excitement grew as they learned of their importance.

Depending on his mood, Jack could make the pumpkins feel happy with some stories, and sad with others. He even told a few scary stories. Most of these came from times in his past when he was afraid, cold, and alone. He liked to tell happy stories, the tales that brought him through the hardest situations in his life. What the other pumpkins did not know, there was time enough for scary stories. The pumpkins best days would draw to a close sooner than they knew.

"Hey Jack," called Autumn Gold one night. She was a beautiful pumpkin, more golden than orange, and she only had eyes for Jack. "Tell us a good story," she asked in a sultry voice.

"Well, it's almost Independence Day," Jack said. "The Fourth of July is a holiday for people. They have picnics, they stay home from work, they attend carnivals, and at night, after dark, they watch fireworks."

Jack explained what it would look like. He told the others that the family would come to the garden and choose one pumpkin to take with them to the festivities. The chosen one got to decorate the picnic table during the feast, ride the Ferris wheel at the carnival, and sit on the blanket under the stars watching the fireworks explode and sparkle in the night sky. Autumn Gold seemed to sparkle herself after listening to Jack's story.

"Do you think they'll choose me?" she asked him.

"You never know," Jack answered.

On the Fourth of July, the farmer and his wife came to the garden and selected several ears of corn from the stalks, a basket of tomatoes, four onions, a handful of lettuce leaves, and a colander full of beets. Pumpkins were not chosen.

"They didn't choose any of us, Jack, not one," Autumn Gold complained. "They even harvested those ugly beets and smelly onions. How could you be so dishonest? I thought we meant more to each other than that," and she didn't speak to Jack until the next month. Jack wondered if he should just stop telling stories.

"Tell us a good one, Jack," Baby Boo said one night. Baby Boo was small and the only white pumpkin in the patch. He was often teased by the other pumpkins because he was different. Baby Boo was the only pumpkin his vine produced. Jack felt for the little guy and tried to make him happy.

"The farmer and his family go on vacation to the beach each year," Jack said. "They come to the patch and choose a pumpkin to take with them on the trip. That pumpkin gets to ride in the car, swim in the ocean, build sand castles, and lie in the sun on a beach towel watching the ocean waves ebb and flow on the sand."

"Aah," said the collection of pumpkins together, imagining all those things.

"Do you think they'll pick me?" asked Baby Boo.

"You never know," said Jack.

Vacation time arrived. The farmer and his family came out to the garden to harvest some vegetables for their journey. They chose squash, cucumbers, green beans, and tomatoes. They didn't choose a pumpkin. The family talked at length about their beach plans. They asked a neighbor to water the garden and help themselves to anything ripe. The farmer, his wife, and children, all walked out of the gate and were gone for a week.

"You said they'd take one of us," said Baby Boo in disappointment. "You lied Jack. How could you be so mean?"

334

Jack didn't want to lie, but he liked happy stories best, ones with fun and warmth. He didn't like to think about the future. He kept those stories to himself.

One night, the farmer came out and walked through the pumpkin patch. The garden breathed quickly and it captured Jack's attention. Something was up. The farmer lifted some of the larger pumpkins a few inches off the ground, Jack being one of them.

"Jack, I love your size, but you're a bit lopsided," the farmer said, "must have been that long winter lying on your side, like you did. Too bad. I think you'd win the ribbon."

The farmer went back in the house after weighing and measuring several of the biggest pumpkins.

"Hey Jack," called Big Max. Big Max was the biggest specimen in the garden, other than Jack. The farmer had spent a long time with Big Max, lifting him onto a scale and winding a measuring tape around his girth, careful not to damage his vine.

"What's going on with the farmer? What's all the fuss about?"

"Well," Jack said, "every September there's the County Fair down the road. The farmer comes out to the garden and chooses

335

one pumpkin to take to the fair. That pumpkin is washed and polished and put on a wooden display rack in the vegetable tent for the people to come and see. Other farmers bring their pumpkins, and the biggest, best looking pumpkin, gets a blue ribbon and their picture in the newspaper."

"Yeah, sure it does, Jack," Big Max groaned. "I'll believe it when I see it."

All the other pumpkins agreed with Big Max. They turned their backs on Jack and stopped talking to him. This made Jack mad. He'd spent his whole summer sharing his wisdom, helping his patch mates understand how things work. And he kept a secret. Jack saved them the heartbreak of finding out their future. He sacrificed his own integrity to make them happy, and this was the thanks he got. Well, he wouldn't take their feelings into account again. Jack's heart turned to pulp.

A few weeks later, the farmer walked into the garden with several bushel baskets. The pulse of the garden seemed to change, its breath grew rapid. The farmer carefully went over every vine in the garden, selecting the very best ears of corn, heads of cabbage, beets, onions, green beans, butter beans, cucumbers, yellow squash, zucchini, and cantaloupe. He loaded the baskets and put them on the back of the wagon.

"See," Big Max said. "I told you, not one pumpkin."

"Yeah," said Autumn Gold and Baby Boo at the same time.

"You're nothing but a liar, Jack," said Funny Face, a bright orange pumpkin with a perfect shape.

Jack sighed. "Just wait," he said, "you'll see. I know more than you think I do."

In about an hour, the farmer and his oldest son came out to the garden and carefully sliced Big Max's vine from his stem. Together, they hefted him up and carried him out of the garden. He was placed in the wagon with the other vegetables.

Jack didn't say, "I told you so." He didn't offer an explanation. He let the others stew in their own juices. Jack stayed quiet. He stayed quiet for over a week.

Big Max returned with a blue ribbon tied around his stem. The farmer and his son brought Big Max back to the pumpkin patch and took his picture with a camera.

"Hey, Jack," the blue ribbon winner apologized, "I'm sorry I doubted you. I've been to the Fair and it happened just like you said. You were right. It was a beautiful week."

"Congratulations, Big Max," said Jack, "the ribbon looks good on you."

"Thanks," said Big Max. The farmer and his son hoisted Big Max again and said they were going to display him in the front yard for everyone to see.

"We'll sell lots of pumpkins when people see we've won this ribbon," the farmer said.

"Bye, Big Max," Jack said. "Hope we get to see you again sometime."

It was late September, and the days were getting shorter. Most of the pumpkins had grown into good sized orange rounds. Jack was still the largest, and so large that some men who came to the patch attempted to lift him, but couldn't.

The other pumpkins tried to get Jack to tell more stories, yet his heart wasn't in it. He gave excuses and encouraged others to take up the hobby of storytelling. Trick or Treat, one of the tall

338

pumpkins on the other side of the patch, tried, but couldn't quite get the knack. He told boring tales of arguments between the hybrid and heirloom pumpkins, or an incident where the farmer's wife tripped with the clothes basket, fell in a heap, and stomped back into the house to re-wash the clothes after she wallowed around on them. The stories would have been funny, except everyone had already witnessed them first hand.

"Please tell us another story, Jack," Baby Boo begged one night.

Jack didn't have any happy stories left. He didn't want to tell another story and he certainly didn't want to tell the scary stories he knew.

"I don't think so," said Jack.

"We're sorry we ignored you, Jack," said Autumn Gold.

"It's not that—" Jack trailed off.

"What is it then?" asked Funny Face.

"I only have scary stories left," said Jack, "and you don't want to hear those."

"Yes we do, Jack. We want to hear scary stories. It's been so long since you've told us a story. Please Jack, please tell us a scary story—please," pleaded Baby Boo.

"OK," said Jack and he thought he heard a sharp breath from the garden. He ignored it.

"It's almost Halloween," he began, "and Halloween is the scariest time of year. People lose all control during this holiday. October begins soon, when the weather gets colder. After the first frost and during the harvest moon, the farmer will come with his sharp knife and cut your vine."

"Cut our vines?" The others asked.

"Yes," answered Jack, "one day, he will walk the patch with a long, sharp knife, hunting pumpkins for harvest. He will come up from behind, and when you least expect it, he'll sever you from your vine, leaving just a stump at your top, like he did with Big Max. He will pick you up, load you onto the wagon, and prepare you for the night of terror."

"Terror? What do you mean terror?" Baby Boo asked. "Big Max got to go to the Fair. He got a blue ribbon. He gets to be on display in the front yard."

"Besides," said Autumn Gold, "the farmer wouldn't harm us. We're special."

"I told you, people lose control at Halloween. I've been around a long time. I've seen things, you know," said Jack.

"We don't believe you, Jack," said Happy Face. "You've told us lies before."

Jack could hear the uncertainty in their voices. They weren't sure. Jack didn't want to say anymore. As he watched their fear grow, he felt bad. He shouldn't have gone this far. He shouldn't have let Baby Boo sway his resolve. Jack grew very quiet. The garden rustled with anxious leaves. Jack wished he could turn back time. He knew their curiosity would get the better of them. He knew they wanted to know their future, no matter how horrible it sounded. They wanted to know the outcome.

"Where will he take us once he cuts us from the vine, Jack?" asked Baby Boo, with a shiver in his whisper.

Jack decided then that if he was in their place, he'd want to know the truth, too. He knew the horror and it wasn't fair to hide it from them. Jack had heard the farmer and his wife talk about it.

"He takes you to—the Farm Stand."

341

"What's the Farm Stand?" Autumn Gold gasped.

"It's a place in front of the farmer's house. He will put you on display and sell you to people for Halloween."

"Sell us to people—for Halloween? Why?" Funny Face asked.

"It's a holiday for people," Jack said, his voice deepening with emotion. Then he paused, gathering his courage, "but not for pumpkins."

"What do you mean?" asked the other pumpkins, the pitch of their voices rising.

Jack started, "Halloween is hideous. Horrible things happen to pumpkins on Halloween. Most do not survive." Then he stopped, afraid to continue.

These pumpkins were his friends, but they'd never understand. They'd blame him for their fate. Jack felt the change in the seasons. Summer was gone. He remembered it from the previous year. The nights were colder now.

"Well don't stop there," Autumn Gold whispered. "What horrible things? We have a right to know."

Last year, the farmer's family members came to the garden for first choice of pumpkins, before the farmer harvested them to sell. The patch listened to the farmer's tales in disbelief. The accounts were terrifying and left them all shaking in fear. Jack remembered, feeling the hairs rise on his vine. He never knew for sure whether the stories were true, but the other pumpkins of the patch screamed in horror as they were taken. Jack had never known the farmer to lie, either.

"Come on Jack, you have to tell us. What will the people do with us on Halloween? What will happen?" asked Baby Boo.

Jack took a deep breath and let it out slowly. He felt the tendrils around his seeds curl and he thought he might be sick.

"Well," he hesitated, feeling flushed even as the night grew cooler.

"Go on, go on," Funny Face encouraged him.

"Well," Jack began again, "some of you will be carved with knives. People gut you, slice chunks out of you to make a scary face, then put a burning candle inside your hollowed out carcass. You sit at the front of the house on Halloween night to scare children."

There was a pause in the garden.

"Oh, how awful. To be tortured and then made to scare children. Who thought of this Halloween anyway?" The pumpkins began to speak together.

"People," Jack said.

He didn't tell the other pumpkins that he was special. He didn't tell them he'd be spared.

"You said they'd do other things, Jack. What other things?"

"Some of you will be peeled, your flesh cut into pieces, cooked, mashed and baked in an oven. People will eat you."

Some of the pumpkins began to cry. Murmurs and moans erupted in the patch. Jack even thought a few lost some of their color. Jack took another breath, so he could finish.

"Teenagers sometimes steal pumpkins from front porches on Halloween night and smash them to bits in the street—where cars run over what's left. And, for those who have been spared torture, once the season is over, pumpkins are rolled down the hill behind the house and left to rot under briers while mice and other scavengers gnaw at your flesh and nibble your seeds."

"You can't be serious, Jack," said Autumn Gold.

344

Jack felt smaller than Baby Boo. If only they hadn't persisted. If only he hadn't known the truth. He wished at that moment that he was as naive as the rest of them. For the first time in his life, he wished to be alone. What had he done to his friends?

Jack watched Baby Boo. The small pumpkin looked even tinier than usual, sitting there, all alone on his own vine, with no one to comfort him. Jack wanted to take it all back, to tell them it was all a lie.

He whispered, "It's the truth."

"Don't believe him," said a voice from the other side of the patch. "You've believed him before, and he's lied to you." It was Trick or Treat, one of the tall pumpkins.

"That's right," said Autumn Gold. "He's lied before."

"It can't be true," came Baby Boo's small voice.

"He's just trying to scare us into thinking he knows more than we do," said Funny Face.

All the pumpkins began talking at once, trying to convince themselves and each other that Jack was wrong. Trick or Treat had planted the seed.

"What I think," said Trick or Treat, "is that Halloween is the grand holiday just for pumpkins and Jack wants to scare us, keep us away from the festivities. Look around you. All the other vegetables have been harvested. We are the only ones left. There must be a reason. I bet the farmer's saving us for the biggest party of the year. Independence Day, Vacation, and the County Fair were just small change compared to our party. I think the Farm Stand is a happy place. Why, I bet the farmer and his family harvest us, dress us in fine clothes, decorate their house in shades of orange, dance with us and treat us like kings and queens. We've spent a long hot summer in this dirt for a reason, and it's not to be carved up, eaten, smashed, or gnawed."

"Yeah," said Funny Face. "He's right—Trick or Treat is right. Don't believe what Jack says. He thinks he's the farmer's favorite. He just wants to leave us out of the fun. He wants us to be afraid so we won't go to the party. He believes he's the king, but he's not."

Jack didn't defend his honor. He didn't want to take away their dreams. He longed for a fancy party, where his compatriots dressed in fine clothes. He wanted all of them to be crowned in a grand coronation, like in the stories of the farmer's granddaughter. He knew better though, and sat quietly as his friends shunned him. Jack fell asleep, a dejected and lopsided pumpkin.

That very night, the sky was clear and the weather turned dreadfully cold. At first light, a sheen of frost coated each pumpkin. They all shivered under its sparkle. The pumpkins whispered among themselves.

A sudden breath from the garden awakened Jack. The farmer and his wife opened the gate and the hinges screeched. The couple held sharp knives. They began harvesting the pumpkins, one after another. The couple moved each one carefully in the wheelbarrow and then lifted it onto the wagon behind the tractor. Some of the pumpkins talked about the party they might attend, while others were quiet. A few cried and screamed. The farmer and his wife talked in low voices and pointed here and there. When the harvest was complete, the only pumpkins left on their vines were Jack, Autumn Gold, Baby Boo, Happy Face, and Trick or Treat.

"Why do you think he left us here?" Autumn Gold asked Trick or Treat. She had stopped talking to Jack.

"Because we're the best of the bunch," answered Trick or Treat.

"Do you really think so?" asked Baby Boo.

"I know so, Boo," said Trick or Treat.

"What happened to the others?" Happy Face asked.

"They're helping to decorate the party," said Trick or Treat. "Planning and creating the biggest party of the year takes some time."

Three long weeks passed while the remaining pumpkins wondered about their fate. Why were they still in the patch? And who was telling the truth? The farmer still came out to the garden and checked on them like he always had. Autumn Gold, Baby Boo, Happy Face, and Trick or Treat formed a tight bond, talking well into the night, supporting one another, and uplifting each other's spirits. If the farmer was still protecting them from harm, maybe it was to keep them. The group ignored Jack, who waited on their fate in silence. Halloween was yet to come.

One crisp morning, the farmer and his wife came out to the garden.

"This one here's for carving," the farmer said, pointing to Happy Face.

"That little white one can sit next to him on the porch tonight," the farmer said, motioning to Baby Boo. The farmer took out his sharp knife and came toward the two pumpkins.

"No, no, please don't!" screamed Happy Face.

"No, not me, not me," cried Baby Boo, "I'm too little."

Jack, Autumn Gold, and Trick or Treat watched in horror as the farmer and his wife cut the two pumpkins off their vine and carried them into the house. The three pumpkins remaining in the patch listened as Happy Face begged, pleaded, and wailed until, some minutes later, he fell silent.

They could still hear Baby Boo sobbing, repeating in his tiny voice, "No, no, no. Why did you do it, why? He was my friend. Why were you so mean?" Jack cried right along with Baby Boo. He no longer wanted to be the farmer's darling. He wanted his friends back. He wanted summer again. Even the stark cold of winter was better than this.

The screen door squeaked as the farmer's wife came out of the house with a knife in one hand and a large metal bowl in the other. She walked slowly toward the pumpkin patch. Her hair hung loose from the scarf on her head and gray strands covered her face. She blew them away from her narrowed eyes. Her face was smeared with pumpkin juice. Her hands and dress were stained with pulp, seeds, and what could only be the entrails of Happy Face. She set down the bowl and unchained the gate. The garden held its breath.

Jack and the others tried to glance into the bowl. They couldn't see over the rim. The farmer's wife picked up the bowl and stepped into the garden. She walked over to the compost pile and emptied parts and pieces of Happy Face into the rotting leaves, and egg shells, and peelings. All that was left of their friend were some seeds, a few jagged chunks of flesh and stringy innards. They felt their own insides turn and tangle. Their vines constricted and they felt dizzy. All three shivered, waiting as the woman slowly turned toward them. She walked to Autumn Gold and bent over.

Autumn Gold screamed in terror. She wailed and yelled, and never stopped screaming until she too, was silenced once inside the house. An hour later, Jack and Trick or Treat smelled cooked pumpkin flesh as it simmered on the stove then baked in the oven.

Neither of the two pumpkins said anything. There were no more stories to tell. They each awaited their fate.

Late that night, Jack heard the rumble of a car on the street. The moon was high and the hour was close to midnight. The car stopped in front of the farmer's house. Then Jack heard young voices—teenagers.

"There's two pumpkins on the porch right there," a voice said.

"Yeah, I'll keep watch, you go grab 'em," another said.

"Not me, Earl. You go do it," the first one said.

"Ya'll ain't got no guts," another voice said. "Give ol' Earl a job, and it gets done," it said.

Jack listened to someone grunt and pick up what was left of Happy Face and all of Baby Boo.

Baby Boo was crying and hollering again, "No, no, no, please don't do it. Don't throw me. Noooo!"

Baby Boo's voice arced through the air and then Jack heard two distinct smacks as pumpkins hit pavement. The voices laughed. Car doors slammed and a vehicle roared off. Jack heard the thump of pumpkin rind hit the curb and land with a crunch in the ditch. He imagined the tires mashing parts and scattering bits of his friends.

The rest of Jack's night stretched long and dark.

The farmer wasn't finished. The next morning he and his wife came to the garden. They sliced through Trick or Treat's vine and lifted him into the wheelbarrow. Then they came over to Jack.

"Gosh," the farmer said, "I hate to harvest him. He's lasted two seasons and he's still going strong. No way he'll last through winter this year. He's too big and his vine's too brittle. We'll collect his seeds, though. You're one hearty pumpkin, Jack old boy. I wish you could have won that blue ribbon. You deserve it for all you've been through."

With that, the farmer took out his knife and sliced through Jack's vine, leaving a stem bleeding a trickle of sap.

The farmer and his wife hefted Jack into the wheelbarrow and the two of them wrestled him into the house and onto the kitchen table. The farmer's wife brought Trick or Treat in a few minutes later and laid him beside Jack.

Trick or Treat was quiet, but Jack could sense his fear as they sat on the table.

Jack wasn't frightened anymore. He knew his fate and rested. His friends had suffered and it wasn't fair to their memory for Jack to worry over his own life.

Jack looked around. He'd always wondered what the inside of the house was like. The temperature was warm, like summer, but Jack felt a chill. He recognized some of the odors that wafted out to the garden. The smells were stronger here—no vegetables that he could discern, but definitely cantaloupe and egg, and maybe a trace of pig. Mid-day and night time smells were different, each with their own aroma. Jack recognized a hint of Autumn Gold lingering in the air.

"Did you see how good the pie turned out?" The woman asked the farmer, holding up a dark, orange disk. She brought it over and placed it close to Jack.

"Yep, looks good," the farmer said, "believe I'll try me a slice after I get the seeds out of these two."

"I know why you want Jack's seeds," said the wife, "but why the other one?"

"That's full of seed passed down from my Granddaddy's pumpkin. I'm choosing this tall one to carry on the family tradition."

The farmer had the knife in his hand, running it over a gray stone. Every so often, he would stop and run his thumb over the blade. Then he'd go back to scratching the knife against the stone. Jack watched, fascinated by the sound and movement, wondering how the blade would feel, slicing into his rind.

Trick or Treat finally spoke up. "Jack?"

"Yeah?" Jack said.

"I'm really sorry I doubted you—and turned the others against you."

"It's OK," Jack said. "I'm glad you gave them some hope. It's more than I did. I'll never forgive myself for that."

"Hey, you were just trying to be truthful. I was the one who lied to them," said Trick or Treat.

"If I had it to do over again, I'd have lied, too. Besides, you didn't know any better," said Jack.

"Yes I did," Trick or Treat said. "I knew you were telling the truth, but I wanted to tell stories just like you. I want you to know, it has been a real privilege knowing you, Jack."

"You too, Trick or Treat. Maybe our vines will meet up in the garden next season and get to know each other. That would be nice."

"Yeah, it would," Trick or Treat said.

The farmer laid down the knife and reached into a bowl.

"These toasted pumpkin seeds are right good," he said, tossing back a handful.

Suddenly, the farmer sputtered, turned red in the face, and clenched his neck. His arm swept across the table in front of Jack, knocking the bowl of seeds and the pie onto the floor with a clatter. He stamped his feet and looked toward his wife. The farmer was turning purple and his eyes rolled back in his head.

The woman came running across the room, but when she reached the farmer, she slipped on the pie and seeds. Her feet shot out from under her and with her mouth opened wide, she let out a screech. Her hands grasped, but found nothing to hold. Her head came down hard on the corner of the table, and she crumpled to the floor.

The farmer began to topple backwards into the glass cabinet against the wall. He crashed, breaking the glass, splintering the

355

shelves, and landed on the floor with dishes and cabinetry piling on top.

Jack and Trick or Treat sat on the table surveying the mayhem. They waited for the farmer and his wife to get up. They did not. The two pumpkins waited, and waited, and waited. Still, the couple never recovered. Their son walked into the house later that night and found the two people deceased. Police and rescue people arrived, loaded the farmer and his wife onto gurneys, then drove them away in wagons with sirens. A man in uniform said the farmer and his wife were dead. Jack and his friend continued to sit on the table, waiting.

"Hey Jack, what do you make of this?" asked Trick or Treat.

"I guess Halloween is over," said Jack.

"What holiday do we celebrate next?"

"Thanksgiving, Trick or Treat. Let me tell you about Thanksgiving—" Jack began.

Outside, the garden sighed and began a winter's sleep.

El Dia de Los Muertos
by Sheila Cano

A blue-black sky turned blood-orange on the horizon as the wind scoured the desert. Ocotillo and prickly-pear cacti loomed in the dusk. Juan thought he saw one moving slowly towards him, but he could not be sure. Weary from a long day in the fields, he saddled his horse to ride back to the tent where Gabriela and his children were camped. He pulled his wool serape close and spurred Pancho on into the autumn night while a golden moon lit the way home. Pancho's hoof-beats echoed hollowly in the silence.

Juan felt something grab his neck, and a hot shiver travelled from the middle of his back across his shoulders to the crown of his head. He twisted around in the saddle and saw a rider close behind, but he heard no hoof-beats. A dark and featureless hooded shape moved atop a horse, blotting out the stars. Juan reined Pancho sharply to face the stranger.

"Who are you? What do you want?"

The rider's eyes, like black mirrors, flashed at him, and Juan heard a sound of swarming bees grow louder until it filled his head.

Go. Go quickly now, or I will stop you forever.

Juan breathed in a ragged gasp and jerked his horse around, digging his spurs into Pancho's sides. Pancho leaped like a deer and galloped hard away. Juan looked back to see the rider following, as closely as the dust swirling up from Pancho's flying hooves, as close as a shadow. Blood pounded in his head.

"Where should I go? If I go home, will my family be killed? Should I lead this rider away? But it will follow me wherever I go. I must go to Gabriela. I must take the chance that we will all be slain. At least we will die together."

Though Pancho sped along, to Juan it seemed as though they were mired in molasses. He slapped the reins and spurred his horse until Pancho was bleeding. Froth whipped from Pancho's mouth, splattering Juan's face. Every time Juan looked back, the figure was floating silently just behind Pancho's tail.

At last Juan saw the lights of the camp. Juan remembered that it was the night before El Dia de los Muertos, the Day of the Dead. There would be a big fiesta at the camp, a bonfire to keep the revellers warm as they danced and sang. Everyone would be happy, some chickens would be killed for the feast, and music would fill the hearts of the villagers. The hardship of living in the desert would be forgotten for a few days as they honored the dead. Pancho slowed as they neared the camp. Juan felt a tremor shake his whole body.

"No! That is no bonfire! Our tent is burning! Gabriela...Gabriela! Los ninos! No, No!"

Juan heard screams. He jumped to the ground while Pancho was still moving. Juan ran to the tent. He saw the shadows of Gabriela and the children. They were waving blankets frantically, trying to put out the fire. The blaze burst through the top of the tent as he reached the doorflap. He lunged inside and seized the baby from Gabriela's arm, grabbed the two eldest children and pulled them outside. Gabriela fled the tent just as it collapsed; sending tall flames and sparks shooting up into the black sky.

They all huddled, panting, weeping. The fear flooding within him eased, and he felt joy rushing through his veins. He laughed and cried all at once, hugging his wife and the children, all covered with soot, smoke stinging their eyes and noses, the baby crying. Just then Juan realized that the rider had vanished. He peered into the night, but saw nothing.

"We must go to the others. They will be at the fiesta. We must tell them we lost our tent, and surely they will help us," Juan said to Gabriela.

"Querido, I was so afraid. We were all asleep, and then I woke to see the flames on the floor. The candle must have fallen over!" Gabriela said. "I had a bad dream. Someone— something—was chasing you."

Juan looked up at the moon, at the stars in the clear dark sky. A tiny shape moved across the moon, grew bigger - a figure on horseback. For a moment the moon disappeared as the shadow expanded, and Juan looked into eyes like black mirrors. He heard the sound of swarming bees inside his head. He breathed in slowly and felt a deep peace spread through his body. He closed his eyes, and when he opened them again, the moon was shining brightly.

"It was a bruja, querida, a witch—a good witch. Tomorrow at the fiesta, we will honor the dead. We will sing to our ancestors, who watch over us."

Read This Please

Volume 1 Edition 6 - Solstice Edition: The Gift

December 21, 2010

Welcome to the final literary edition of ReadThisPlease.com Volume One: The Gift. Let's pull up some comfy chairs again and curl up in that big blanket—because these stories aren't necessarily about bows and presents. It's the Solstice, where we are perched at the apex of a season and begin the change into a new year. Consider the bounty that's been bestowed upon you and where we're going. Onward.

The Silent Pines
by Steven Bird

Bill carried his boots in his hand, not wanting to clunk through the house and wake Ione. The brown, western cut polyester suit fit him too snug. He'd decided he didn't need the necktie. In the kitchen, he poured a cup of yesterday's coffee and heated it in the microwave. He drank the coffee watching the first light of day spread along the flat horizon beyond the kitchen window. An inch of fresh snow covered the ground and lined the bare limbs of trees in the yard. He drank the cup empty and placed it on the table, then pulled an envelope containing a letter from his jacket pocket and propped it against the cup so that it would stand out above the regular clutter of bill and notice envelopes filed on the table.

He pulled his boots on. Took his hat from a peg by the door, walked outside and headed toward the barn. His footsteps crushed the dry snow with a sound like groans. The sky sagged with massed clouds. Signs, he figured, the world was losing its light and a secret foulness ranged afoot. Bad damn luck. He spit.

His figure shifted shapes in the chrome as he passed the pickup parked in the barn, headed for the tack room. He threw a few handfuls of oats into the trough in the paddock, went out to the corral and caught his horse, and saddled it while it finished the oats. He was already leading the sorrel out when he thought of it – and returned to the tack room to fetch his spurs. He fastened the spurs to his boots. Then he led the horse out of the barn with the spur rowels clinking and his breath streaming like smoke from his head in the raw cold. Bill mounted the horse, urged it to a fast walk and rode out across the pasture over snowy ground prone and leached under an injured pink sky. A broken line of cows escaped single file down the distance, their heads bowing and lifting.

Beyond the pasture the land tilted upward and pines assembled along the rise, and he rode up among them following a cow trail, then he hooked off the trail onto a path made by coyotes. The path wound over a rise and down into a draw where an old bullpine stood in the snow like a hefty ranch wife in a dough spattered house dress, its limbs akimbo in a posture of eternal furor against the empty page sky.

He drew the horse to a stop under the tree where there was a stout branch low enough to brush his hat. He took his hat off and tossed it. He unstrung his riata from the saddle and threw the loop over and then reached up and tied the bitter end fast to the branch. He put his head into the loop and drew the honda tight against the back of his neck. The horse stomped a foot and blew. He drew a plastic zip-tie from his pocket, looped it around both wrists and used his teeth to pull the loop closed.

He sat on the horse and looked straight ahead inhaling the scent of pines. A crow lit in the top of a nearby tree sending a spit of snow falling down the branches.

He pulled his feet from the stirrups and the big Spanish rowels of his spurs sawed upwards against the sorrel's loins and the horse leaped forward –

Bill dangled from the branch, snow avalanching from the tree and down onto him. He dangled. The fall was not enough to break his neck. His face turned from red to purple to black and his eyes bulged out onto his cheeks and his bladder let go darkening his pants while his coupled arms went up and down in a chopping motion, faster than they had ever dealt cards, and his feet danced, kicked and danced, faster than they had ever danced at the whorehouses in Ely.

The crow dropped and spread its wings, lifted over the trees disappearing. And Bill hung, his body slowly rotating at the end of the rope, this way, then that way, under the branch in sepulchral light amidst the silent pines.

*

The letter began:

Dear Ione,

You have been a good enough wife and this is not your fault. There is evil in the world and it has got ahold of me and given me habits that a man can't live with...

He confessed everything. The gambling. The women.

But of course she already knew.

*

She'd quit going to church. It didn't seem to do anybody any good. The ranch brought enough to pay off the bills and buy the condo. She loved Hawaii. Waves of the ocean. Flowers. She didn't miss that never-break-even ranch at all. Nothing but work. Cold winters. She forgave Bill for almost everything. Men are fools. She forgave him. But when she thought about it, though she would never admit it out loud, she had to allow that in the end Bill had given her a gift of sorts and she secretly thanked him for that.

Breath

by Sarah Scott

My breath hangs in front of me, suspended in blackness, a white-gray vapor of life dissipated. I breathe in cool fall air, it burns all the way to my lungs. My hands ache beneath cotton gloves in which they are wrapped. I rub them together to warm them up. No use. Everything is beautiful when it's dead. Words that we missed when living, we understand now. Our words travel beyond us, beyond lifetimes. On paper, they remain. Through stories they are passed down to our children, and their children, and our great grandchildren. We pass on the gift, from generation to generation, a heritage of words and thought each surpassing the other. So I smile as my daughter says "Mommy I can see my breath," for I know where those thoughts go and what wonderment they will hold for her when she is older. For now, I am thankful everything is beauty and joy for my princess. Plenty of time later for reflection. Childhood is but a vapor from our lips, extended in a frosty morning then dissipated.

Pigeon Trick
by Bruce Reisner

Like you could put parentheses on either side of the block, the one between Mellon Center and Macy's was set apart from the others by pigeons. They had chosen all skyscrapers, a lot of them on the stately city block, to rest upon. Wise birds. That block provides sills, ledges shoulders, roofs, alcoves, lattice work, and gargoyle installations, all for the pigeons to snuggle up together. It was like the tall buildings had fur on a sunny, perfect, fall day.

The sidewalks were packed, midday afternoon crush, lunch time. As I crossed Smithfield Street to the pigeon coated block, I happened to notice a tall thin man, holding a long white bag in one hand, smiling, beautifully, beside a fountain at the far end of the city block. No sooner had I come parallel to the first of so many pigeons bobbing on the busy sidewalk, the young man reached into his long white bag, and drew from it the remains of his lunch.

Through my stuffy bifocals I could discern that it was the last third of a foot long hoagie. He broke a piece off of it, and like the maestro of a symphony waving his baton, he threw it underhanded, up, up, up and gracefully down, down, down to no place in particular on the sidewalk. The pigeons closest to it were first responders, hopping and flapping towards the breezing bits of bread. Their work was rewarded for taking initiative, munching away, but not for long. More birds on the side walk moved in for the free lunch. Then some of the birds on the sills and gargoyles flew down, and a small scale riot began, perhaps a few hundred birds fighting over food. The gent in the distance looked much too happy to be working for the cause of world peace, if this was any indication.

On his first toss I realized that my clothes were in danger of being soiled. Pigeons relieve themselves without care or shame, and I fear being under the process. I was advancing on foot towards the epicenter of what was about to happen, feeling trepidation. But the man with the hoagie was smiling so warmly that good cheer had to be factored in. This was looking like a funny situation. People being crapped on by thousands of pigeons is probably funny.

His second and third tossing of the hoagie did it. Thousands upon thousands of pigeons came pouring down from the minion of skyscrapers, all focused on the food and fearless to go for it. The riot that ensued had the force of a tornado, an amicable one, one that has the decency to let you step past it. It was a huge battle among pigeons, and they only beat and pecked at one and other, leaving pedestrians to find their way through the chaos.

My fear of being crapped on escalated, of course, but again, that young man's smile in the distance was more compelling than some petty concern for the threads I had on. It was obvious the gent knew exactly what he was doing. He knew that the power and the glory could tip if he provided the proper impetus. A billion pigeons, some greasy pinched bread, and a symphony composer's vision. The solid crush of birds coming down from high above could have been the forces of fate. The riot in the street, his prank, was magnificent. All that movement brought my senses to life. It was a thrill to walk through birds.

Well, that's all I saw of the young man with the bag of tricks and the mischievous smile. Upon passing the spectacle, I took visual inventory of my hat, jacket, trousers and shoes, and felt gifted to have not a single dropping on my clothes. That, in spirit, is a sign that this happened for all good purposes. It is possible to make things happen.

Chocolate Dreams
by Margaret-Dawn Thacker

I've been sorting recipes. Each one brings back the memory of a sweet or tart taste on my tongue. The sets of instructions in their familiar hand writing tell a story that is richer than the ingredients scribbled on the piece of paper between my fingers. Most are memories of my Grandma standing in her kitchen, my kitchen now. She has an apron tied around her waist and she's pushing her hair off her forehead with the back of her hand. The room is hot, even with the windows up. Grandma doesn't mind or complain. She's measuring, pouring, mixing and humming a tune. She's already made a pound cake and two pumpkin pies. The aroma of vanilla, cinnamon, nutmeg and cloves reminds me of Thanksgiving. It's summer though, and a family reunion is tomorrow in Bath County.

I leave the kitchen table and walk over to the counter where she stirs a sweet mixture in a big shiny green bowl. She's using a wooden spoon and she lifts the bowl, holding it up at an angle to better scrape the sides. She smiles down at me and stops her movement, inviting my small index finger to dip in for a taste.

"What do you think?" she asks.

I put my chocolate covered finger in my mouth and close my eyes. "Mmmm," I say. "My favorite."

"This one's all for you," she says. "No one else is allowed to have a bite, unless you say so."

That's the way my Grandma Payne is. She and I are best buddies. She loves my cousins, but I know she loves me best. She doesn't make Chocolate Dreams for them. Chocolate Dreams are our secret. She makes peanut butter cookies for my cousins. She makes them share.

"I can't wait for tomorrow," I say, remembering all the food and all the fun I have with my cousins. We're going to Uncle Wallace's summer camp cabin on the Jackson River. The men will sit around in folding aluminum chairs, drinking sweet iced tea, while the women get the food together lay it all out on the long pieces of plywood held up by saw horses. The red checked table cloths cover the wood.

We will swim and splash in the cold mountain water until our toes go numb. We'll shiver when we get out, wrapping ourselves in towels and look for a spot of sunshine to warm us between the shade of the trees.

A paper plate never held so many good things as it does at our family reunions. The fried chicken is hot and crisp when I bite into it. Aunt Bertie made this batch, because it has a hint of pepper. Grandma's potato salad is creamy with small crunches of onion and celery. I take out the green pepper. I don't like it. Mama is not so picky about what I have on my plate at a family reunion, so I skip the vegetables in favor of sweeter things, like corn pudding, candied yams, and Aunt Idie's cole slaw which has more sugar than vinegar. There's a whole table of nothing but desserts. My cousins and I sneak as many as we can without getting our hands smacked.

Grandma calls me over to her. It's late afternoon and everyone is stuffed, laid back, some snoozing in their chairs. Most of the food is put away in the trunks of cars for the ride home. Grandma's sitting on the top step of the cabin. She lifts the hem of her apron and wipes her face. She's been busy inside, washing dishes and preparing leftovers for the return trip home. She and Aunt Ruby, Aunt Connie, Aunt Ellen, and Aunt Hallie have exchanged recipes for new dishes that were good.

I look up at her. "Yes Ma'am?"

She motions for me to lean in close. "If you go to the car, there's a round green tin in the backseat floorboard. Your

Chocolate Dreams are in there." She winks at me and gets up to go back inside.

I wander over to the car by myself, open the door and find the tin of Dreams. I lift the top and take one out, biting it, savoring the taste of chocolate, letting it melt and go down slowly. Folding the wax paper back over the treats, I close the box and put it back where I found it. For a second, I feel guilty about my secret, but only for a second. I won't tell them. My cousins can be content with peanut butter cookies.

Texting God
by Adrienne Moody

I am a recovering Catholic. I was brought up with this weathered brick colored catechism book that is still to this day imprinted into my mind. Impure thoughts and impure touching, according to this rule book, is a sin to be confessed and penance given by a white-robed man on the other side of the confessional. I can say this now and fear not that lightning will strike me: My best fantasies were whilst putting in my time at Mass. Okay, I did look upwards after that sentence.

My brother was an altar boy. During Lent one year on the same day that Our Lord carried the cross, he and two fellow altar boys carried a wooden cross 20 miles and got their picture on the front page of the gazette. The next year he discovered girls, alcohol and marijuana, in that precise order. Soon after these life-altering discoveries, he and his buddies were caught in the Church's altar in the middle of the night breaking into the wine used for communion to wash down the host representing the body of Christ. Yikes!

I envy those who pray fiercely, their eyes squeezed shut and lips moving reciting the ancient prayers used to summon the Lord, who apparently will listen and deliver to the devout. I envy them their peace of mind that I know they have, knowing someone cares up there and has the power to change it all. Faith is everything isn't it? I've never had it. And I really, really tried.

I went to church in my little seaside town about five years ago. I missed my deceased parents and went hoping to recapture....something of them. They were practicing Catholics right to their last days. In fact, just before my dad received last rites he mentioned to me that he wanted to tell the priest that he never ever agreed on the decision to allow Catholics eat meat on Fridays. This astounded me; why would he care about something as minor as that? Couldn't he think of something more profound to ponder during his last days?

I digress. I sat in the back pew and decided to text my son before the Mass started. Midway through my message to him, an acquaintance appeared suddenly in my face and she whispered to me, "God doesn't have a cell phone... he won't hear you." I know she was appalled that I would display such dishonor to Him in His House, but I just smiled back at her, fearless, and pressed SEND.

When I speak of such things: my lack of faith in God, I do admit that descending to the ground in a plane with engine failure, my thoughts would be: 'I believe! God help me!' But those words are of desperation and probably originate from my childhood brainwashing.

My Buddhist friend told me that the Dali Lama at the beginning of a documentary about Buddhism states simply this: 'Buddhism will not save you.' He did this knowing that the film would be viewed by curious Christians and he wanted this known right up front: If you're looking to be saved look elsewhere.

I like that honesty.

I'm not saying I have the potential to be a devout Buddhist, but at least it's honest. And as the Church continues to deny and hide the men who have committed one of the worst crimes against children, I let my membership to Catholicism expire permanently.

The Parting Gift

by Adrienne Moody

(Mature: some coarse language)

My Father's death nearly broke my brother. It devastated all of us but it nearly destroyed Cameron, the eldest in our family. We teased him calling him, "The Golden Boy." No doubt he was my parent's favorite: handsome, athletic, sharp witted and possessed high intellect. He excelled in all that he did and rebounded many times. He skied bare-foot, paid much of his University tuition playing snooker at the pool hall near campus, took off to Inuvik and worked for a year to think over his future and bank some money to support his focused plans. Women flocked to him and I could see why. Although he was not a tall man, he was strong but rather than using brute strength to get what he wanted, his sharp mind could twist you up and you'd mentally cry, "Uncle!"

The famous picture of James Dean walking in the rain hunched over and hands in his pockets looked very similar to Cameron.

Boulevard of Broken Dreams.

Cameron lost everything during the real estate crash years ago. He built five deluxe homes in a new sub-division and barely put the for sale signs up when we experienced the worst crash in decades. I paid a visit home during that time; my two older brothers were the only remaining children living in our home town. He was a different man. The fire in him was all but gone. I filled in with the one-liners that evening and I could tell it grieved him that he could not keep up, that his mind was dulled with his losses.

"It shouldn't have happened," was his response when I asked him about the bank's takeover of his properties.

He did everything right. No one could have predicted the real estate crash and how people could no longer afford their mortgages and were walking away from their financial responsibilities.

My Mother often said things that were inappropriate and her words dug at our self esteem. She told Cameron that she thought Lewis, the middle brother, could get him a job at the post office. His response was the clicking sound of the phone hanging up in her ear.

"Call him, Roger," she begged my Father.

"Why did you say that, Mom? You know how he feels about Lewis. You insulted him," I said to her, exasperated.

"What's wrong with working there? He's lost everything and now he wants to take his family and move away! Call him, Roger."

My mother quit smoking and she replaced her addiction with Cheezies. At first it was certs, but because of the vast amounts she consumed, the Retsyn burned her throat so badly the doctor ordered her to stop chewing them. Any sign of stress and the Cheezies came out.

"There's nothing wrong with what I suggested," she insisted pushing another couple into her mouth and dialed his number again. "He's taken the phone off the hook. Go over there, Roger."

My Dad complied and the first thing he saw was the garage door was seriously damaged. His wife told him that Cam had driven his car into it earlier in the day. She was sobbing.

He opened Cam's bedroom door and saw him on the bed with the covers piled on top of him. The drapes were pulled.

"Cam, we're worried about you," my Dad spoke tentatively.

"Get the fuck out of my house! Now!"

My Father did and reported back to us that there really was nothing we could do. Subsequently, within a couple of months, Cam moved his family eight hundred miles away and he started over. No one spoke of his bankruptcy and in a very short time he owned two homes and a thriving lumber and hardware store. Cameron demonstrated his resiliency. We, once more, were in awe of him.

Then the news came that Dad had lung cancer from years of smoking. Cameron could not accept that he was dying. We all knew. Lung cancer and emphysema will take you swiftly. Eight months was all my dad had. I flew home often and now my brother lived only miles from me. I met up with him at the airport the last flight I took while my dad was still alive. I was going up the escalator and he was going down.

"Hey!" I called out to him.

We had a chance to talk, briefly.

"Where are you going?" he asked.

"Home to see Dad."

"You know, Adrienne, It's all mind over matter. He's got a terrible attitude. Every time I call him he tells me the same thing. When I ask him how he is, he says, 'Oh, about the same.' I'm sick of the same old song and dance from him. You know what I told him a couple of days ago?"

"No, what?"

"I told him if he says that one more time, I'm not going to call him anymore."

My Father died two weeks later. The family gathered at the funeral home where his body was displayed for us to pay our last respects. We expected Cam to lead us somehow, to show us how to deal with this loss as he always demonstrated superior leadership qualities.

He told us to please leave him and Mom alone in the viewing room as he had something important to discuss with her. We left thinking it was his first step in taking charge of the dire situation. After twenty minutes my sister finally opened the door a crack to peer in and saw Cam's head on our Mom's lap. He was sobbing and she comforted him by stroking his hair and speaking softly.

We knew in that moment we were on our own and Cameron was dethroned. In the weeks and months that followed each of us learned what strengths we had and it took my Father's death for us to realize them. Cam was the Executor of the Will and when my youngest sister handed him a box of documents that needed to be signed and dealt with he shrugged his shoulders and told her to just throw them in the garbage. He caught a flight home the next day. My sister prolonged her visit by two weeks to tie up all the business that needed to be tended to.

Like mopping up after a disaster, that is what we did.

We learned that relying on someone else to look after us was a mistake. Perhaps for the first time in our lives we learned to act within our family without the eldest overseeing and critiquing.

"Golden Boy, indeed," we muttered often as we took on yet another chore to finish off the burying of the dead. After we all returned home and began the healing process I realized the next step would not be an easy one and that was learning to forgive Cam for caving in on us, for leaving us to do all the dirty work.

But I know now that all that transpired was really a gift.

Trial By Fire

by Margaret-Dawn Thacker

I spent half of my childhood at Rock Mills in Ivy, Virginia. Catharine and Kerry Gilmer were my best friends. They lived there. My mother was friends with their mother, Phyllis. Our Grandmothers were friends as well. Our children are now friends. It's a family tradition, these connections between us.

Rock Mills had a sign like all the other farms on Rt. 637, only it was smaller and more rustic. "The Rocks", "Rosemont", and "Langford" had signs with gold and green lettering. They were professionally made. The one at Rock Mills was more like a name plate. It was about a foot long and nailed to a small wooden post in the ground. Kerry burned the letters into the wood in shop class at school and painted white around the edges. It wasn't fancy, but captured hearts like a plaster hand print of a five year old.

The driveways leading to the other farms were paved and wide. Rock Mills' driveway was gravel in some parts, and worn down dirt in others which turned to mud in the snow and rain. The driveway was over a mile long and so narrow that you had to back up if you met someone coming out when you were coming in. There were two pull-over spots that worked if the two cars were small. Trucks didn't have a chance.

Every trip to Rock Mills was an adventure. The farmhouse there was as plain as the sign and the driveway. Its white bulk was a rectangular box with no porch. Originally, the house had been a large log cabin with two rooms, one stacked on top of the other. Those were now the living and dining rooms, sixteen feet wide and thirty two feet long. Both had rock fireplaces, initially used for heat and cooking. The kitchen was added later, adjacent to the dining room. The biggest bedroom and bathroom were put in over the kitchen, and when they set the top floor over it all, the house gave birth to three more bedrooms. "It has character," my mother said, "a life and history all its own." Kerry told me once that the foundation was built by slaves living on the property before the Civil War. The house was hot in summer and cold in winter. The front door was nailed shut and when you stood at the side of the house and looked up, there was a storm door with no steps or porch under it. It just stood there like someone forgot about it.

"We could invite Billy Hughes over," I told Kerry and Catharine once.

"Why would you want to invite that bully over?" Kerry asked me.

"We could show him to that door when it was time to go home." We all laughed and called it The Bully door from then on.

The only television in the house could get one fuzzy channel when it rained. We had plenty to keep us busy outside though. We waded the creek, fished in the pond, and sat in the old 1952 Black Chevy in the open lean-to barn. The three of us took turns driving our imaginations over the Rockies to California. If time was running short, we didn't leave Virginia. We just imagined day trips to the beach or to Culpepper County, where there was an amusement park with a Ferris wheel. We built wooden go carts and raced them through the pasture, hoping we didn't lose a wheel and land in a cow pie.

Summers were most fun, but winters brought snow. I got snowed in at Rock Mills, one winter. I didn't leave for a week. It took three days with a tractor's front end loader to plow the driveway. With fences on either side and drifts piled, there was no place to push the snow. It had to be picked up in the loader and dumped over the bridges into the creek. The men in the family took turns getting cold on the tractor. We kids played in the snow until we ran out of dry clothes, then we'd sit at the kitchen table by the wood stove and sip hot chocolate while curtains of blue jeans, sweatshirts, socks, long underwear, hats, scarves and mittens hung around us from a drying line.

I liked making snow angels, snowmen, and snow ice cream. I never liked sledding. It scared me. Creeks lived at the bottom of hills and when the sled runners overshot the bank, I pitched over into the frigid water where I scraped my hands, knees and face on sharp rocks. When Kerry's dad and uncle started talking about having a sledding party two nights after the big snow, I imagined another terror, sliding into the creek in the dark.

Everyone was excited, but me. I had two choices. I could sit alone in the house, reading, or stand on the hill shivering, while chicken noises prompted me to try to ignore the fear and take the dark plunge down the steep hill behind the farmhouse. No one I knew ever went sledding at night. I wondered what was wrong with these people who usually seemed so normal.

Mr. Gilmer came inside, stamping his feet and flinging water droplets from his hat and coat. "You kids get on your boots and coats and come with me," he said to us. We followed him outside. I need y'all to take the sled to the wood pile and load it up with kindling. Bring it back over here and put it in that box on the other side of the fence for the bonfire tonight." I'd never seen a bonfire, didn't know what one was.

386

"What's a bonfire?" I asked.

"Honey, it's the biggest outdoor fire you've ever seen. We piled up some brush here last week when we heard the storm was coming. We'll add some wood to it and when we light it, we'll brighten up the night. When you get cold, from sledding and tubing, you can come up the hill and warm your backside at the fire."

"We'll roast hot dogs and marshmallows, too, make S'mores," Catharine said.

"We'll have hot chocolate out here too. You haven't lived until you've been to one of our sledding parties," Kerry said.

This was sounding better. I could take a long time roasting my hot dog and eat more than one S'more, sip my hot chocolate and make it last. I could drag out the eating part until the sledding part was over.

We gathered the kindling and helped carry the rest of the firewood. Then we followed Mr. Gilmer to the shed. He unlocked the door and there were two large, inflated inner tubes made for tractor tires and two more smaller ones for trucks. "These," he said, "are for tonight. They fly."

"Yeah, they fly," Kerry said, his face looking like the thought of that speed was something he dreamed about.

"It's fun," Catharine said, putting a hand on my shoulder. "You'll see."

"I don't like the creek," I said.

"Oh we don't go into the creek, Margaret. We sled and tube into the pond," Kerry announced.

"The Pond?" Now, I imagined drowning in ice water, which was far worse than scraped knees. "Well count me out, I'm not drowning," I said.

"The pond is frozen solid, Margaret. It's only a breeding pond for trout, not deep. You can't fall through and there's a fence on the other side that stops you," Mr. Gilmer said. "Nothing to worry about."

Sure, I thought. Nothing to worry about, taking flight on an inner tube, over a pond, which might be frozen, and if I did make it across the pond without crashing through, I hit a fence. Sounded like fun. "OK," I said.

They lit the bonfire at dark. It was the biggest fire I ever saw, large and round at the bottom with flames licking way up into the night. Sparks shimmered and flickered, falling down from the sky, and sizzling out in the snow. I roasted my hot dogs, made S'mores, sipped hot chocolate and waited my fate. I was almost out of time. Everyone was getting ready to tube.

Earlier, Mr. Gilmer made a track down the hill to the pond, by putting Kerry and Catharine on the edges of the inner tube and walking them down the hill, guiding the round black ring in the direction of the pond. He tried to get me to sit with them to make the track, but I wouldn't do it, afraid the thing would get away from him and we would be on a runaway ride of terror. Once the track was forged, Mr. Gilmer settled himself into one of the tubes and gave it a test run. He was right, it went fast down the hill, over the lip of the pond, and halfway across. He jumped up, stomped around the pond to show me it was safe and trudged back up the hill carrying the black ring.

My Mama was brave. She never feared anything. The more dangerous it was, the more she liked it. She swam in the ocean when waves knocked her down, drove fast around corners in a 1965 red Mustang, white water rafted on the New River in West Virginia and confronted leather wearing motorcycle riders who flipped her the bird. She was a five foot tall female Captain Courageous. I wanted to be brave, but was too busy bargaining with God to keep her safe to build up my own courage. She

389

would look at me, wink and say "Gotta sink or swim," before running to her next daring act.

Tubing a steep hill, over a frozen pond into a board fence gave a new meaning to "sink or swim." My mother wasn't even there for me to talk to God about. I was on my own. Kerry, Catharine, and all of the adults took turns flying down the hill. Several times they fell off the tube, rolling in the snow and laughing, but no one broke through the ice or broke their neck on the fence.

"Come on Margaret," Kerry and Catharine said. "Ride with us, it's fun. You'll see."

I shook my head. They kept sledding.

Mr. Gilmer was standing next to me while I watched the fire and listened to it crack and pop. "You know you're missing a lot of fun, standing here don't you?" he said to me.

I nodded my head. "I'm just a big chicken," I said quietly.

"It's alright to be scared," he said. "I've been scared plenty of times in my life"

"You were?" I asked.

"Sure, everyone gets scared. Know what I did though?"

"What?" I asked.

"I looked that fear right in its ugly face and yelled, "I'm not letting you get the better of me. I'm bigger, badder and braver than you." Then I give my biggest wolf growl and throw myself at it headfirst." He demonstrated by dropping his head and butting me with it.

He made me laugh when he yelled "bigger, badder and braver" and growled like a wolf.

"Tell you what," he said. "If you will ride just once down that hill on a tube with me, we'll never ask you to do it again. It's OK if you don't, but if you never try Margaret, you'll always wonder how much fun you missed."

Mr. Gilmer was a big man. His arms looked like a safe place to be. He cleared the track of all the other tubers. He sat down in one of the biggest tubes and planted his heavy boots in the snow to anchor. He patted his lap. I dragged my feet over to the side of the tube, turned around and sat on the edge of it. He waited. "Ready?" he asked. I nodded my head and he pulled me over into his lap. He put his wool plaid wrapped arms around me and told me to hang on tight. "OK," he said, "Say it with me." I looked at him with a question on my face. Then he started and I joined in,

"I'm bigger, badder and braver than you," we yelled. Then, we growled that wolf growl and Mr. Gilmer lifted his feet.

We started sliding. My breath caught in my chest. I wanted to close my eyes, but wanted to see where I was going. Part of me wanted to jump off, but the other part won out. Before I had much time to think, we were over the lip of the pond and the back of the tube was bouncing off the fence. We came to a swirling stop at the far edge of the pond. 'I did it," I whispered.

"Take that, fear. You're not so big and bad after all," Mr. Gilmer said.

He took the tube and my hand and we started across the pond to the bottom of the hill. The ice didn't give way, and I didn't drown. I looked up at the fire and Kerry and Catharine were jumping up and down clapping and cheering, so were the adults. I felt fearless.

I took a turn with every adult first, then with my friends, and finally, I took my own tube and let it fly. Kerry's face was right. It was the speed of dreams. I tubed until my limbs got stiff and my toes and fingers were numb. Mr. Gilmer called me over to the fire. "Turn around girl and warm your backside, you're about frozen," he said. We were standing side by side, looking down the hill toward the pond. "Know what we call a night like tonight, Margaret?" he asked me.

"No," I said

"A trial by fire, Margaret, that's what we call it, when we fight our fear and test our belief in ourselves, a trial by fire. You did good."

"Yes sir," I said. "I did good."

Gift of Tears

by B G Lewis

Hearing a whisper chanced
in a feather's frantic tapping,
above the din, tender rapping,
gasping 'neath a window's ledge.

And peering through the garden's
thickest, where nettle and thistle
bury quickest forgotten trinkets
of occasion, ceremony, and might have's,

And kneeling, considering, I cupped it.
Clearly fallen from commonplace,
from song flown into reality,
slipping dire into disregard.

And in a wounded one's stillness
came tears, long lost to fulfillment,
not of fear, but loosened in purity;
on a stumble in death's humble garb.

In regret came the muse wondering,
delightfully draped in obscurity,
charming a seeker to sorrowing
and teasing the silk through the shards,

To glimpse and behold, unfaltering,
as a world fades below golden,
in seasons forever flown splendidly,
on the pillow of the one soul.

Measure of a Life

by Sheila Cano

what is the measure of a life together
gone forever

how a brother died alone
he looked like a dark-haired Jesus
lying on a gurney in the morgue
I had to see him to make sure
to say good-bye
he said he wasn't much of a brother
I said yes you were

how a mother died alone
still warm on the rug
her green eyes open
the glass of milk on the table
she set it down
when she felt her heart burst open
she died before she hit the floor
her dinner in a pool beside her mouth

I am sorry, Mom
I'm sorry you suffered so much

how a first husband died alone
beside the bathtub
the pains in his arms and legs
were not due to the flu after all
his coffin was too small
his shoulders crowded tightly
the wide silver bracelet
held him together
I laid a red rose on his chest

how a second husband died alone
sitting in his chair
the whiskey glass beside him
his green eyes open
his arms mottled blue and red
the pain in his soul stopped
the chair cushion stained
with his last urination
I laid a bluejay feather on his coffin

what is the knowing of a person
a wet dishtowel flicked at me in fun
a dime under my pillow

397

a hand on my hot damp brow
a glance of silent understanding
you know what I am thinking
warmth of a body pressed to mine
hot coffee by the campfire
stars in a black sky
reflected in the lake

when they each return in my dreams
I find out more about them
we talk as if we were still together
not alone forever

The Choice
by Steven Bird

The cabin set in a mossy stand of old firs, back from the road and away from the dust and noise of the log trucks. A small stream where the deer come to drink and steelhead ascend coursed beneath overhanging blackberry and ferns just beyond her door. The sun fresh up over the stark trees shed yellow light through the branches and paint-peeled kitchen window to illuminate the chipped enameled sink, the water stained plank sideboard, a pot of oatmeal on the stove offering up a thin ghost of steam to the raw morning. She ladled some of the oatmeal into a clay bowl. She hummed to herself, not a tune, like a harmonious drone, a soft barely audible resonance emitted from her core like a cat's purr. She was young, just twenty-two and the quiet mystery of the maiden still illuminated her cheek. Her long sorrel hair crested from a prominent cowlick above her temple to fall as a breaking wave around the one errant ear poking through the gold torrent tossed beside the freckled heart shaped face. A country face. The lips more wise than sensuous. She was a thin girl but motherhood had blessed her with a fecund roundness placed lovingly upon her lithe animal frame. Her hips swayed with the morning routine, swinging her print skirt. She stirred a little honey into the cereal.

The baby chirped from his bassinet and at the child's signal a surge came to her breasts, and she went to him and gathered him. He cranked a little still waking up. When his eyes fully opened he recognized her and his cross expression flashed to the self-assured face that babies have knowing they are the center of all affection. She enfolded him, opened her flannel blouse. He sucked hard for a moment then stopped and opened his eyes wide to look at her, then closed them again and resumed, easier, milk drunk, contented. Her body emitted melodic sound and she and the baby moved to the rhythm.

She'd been looking forward to this day. She wanted to make a new blouse and needed some things, and she was driving over to Eugene to shop. She didn't go to town often, maybe once a month. She wasn't a girl who needed to go to town a lot.

It was an hour's drive to Eugene on one of those narrow bent roads that follow twisting rain swollen rivers between the Willamette Valley and the coast. The road winds past small mossy farms with luxuriant green pastures where cattle bow their heads and young horses run and the pastures are fringed with blackberry and Queen Ann's lace. The fields slope to canopied corridors of alder and maple lining the river course and the road.

The world flashing from light to dark to light through the windshield as she and the baby rode under the tree canopy.

She loved horses. She sang to the baby …all the pretty little horses… and the baby sensed more than heard the tune over the engine noise. She rolled her window down half way, enough to let in the tree-dense atmosphere but not so far that there was too much breeze on the baby bundled like a prize pumpkin and strapped into his car seat beside her. He was already asleep. He was a good little baby and a good traveler.

A sunny day is a celebration in Oregon. Sunny days bring folks out, and the people of town were bright and beautiful in the stores and on the sidewalks and assembled on the promenade benches and little parks scattered about the busy town. Pale faces tilted hopefully toward the conquering sun.

Eugene is a friendly walking city and she liked to poke through the downtown notion shops, the baby in his pack riding high and snug against her purposeful back. She'd picked up the embroidery thread needed for the blouse and a few things for the baby.

What a beautiful day, she mused breathing in the scents of water and flowers and the colognes of humanity wafting by on warm drafts. She stopped at a cobbled square. A fountain sent up fluted arcs of water to fall murmuring into a round pool where tossed coins dotted the aqua blue bottom, each holding a wish. A stone rim surrounds the fountain to form a bench where people may sit, and it was pleasant, and she sat to take a rest and give the baby a little juice.

The square was festive and breezy. An earnest guitar player on the other side of the fountain finished tuning his guitar and started to riff, then warmed up and loosed a cascade of jangling notes to fill the brilliant fountain square. He was pretty good, and a few kids gathered to listen. There was a boy with purple hair, and a pretty girl with a ring through one side her nose.

The anomalous suspended hook of a thin daytime moon hung in the blue sky over the fountain. The baby slept on her lap while she cradled him, and she rested tranquil on the fountain bench with him. It felt good to be out in the sun. She thought she would sit for awhile and listen to the music before going for groceries and heading home. A band of pigeons picked their way around the fountain and came right up next to her feet. One made a tentative peck at her sneaker lace. She remained still, wishing she had something to give them.

She noticed the photographer in the square by the fountain. He fired at the pigeons with his camera and the pigeons rose and scattered.

402

She looked away for a moment, and when she looked ahead again he was there in front of her. He'd approached with the sun in her face. She raised a hand to shield her eyes from the glare and get a look at him.

A handsome young man with a halo of wavy brown hair. She thought there may have been a slight insolence in his eyes, but didn't she see that in a lot of faces? Most people, she allowed, are innocent of their impropriety by virtue of their ignorance. Anyway, she didn't like to judge. But he was standing too close, directly at her feet, smiling and pointing to the camera hanging from his neck.

You are so pretty, he said, do you mind if I take your picture?

She smiled at the man, shy, dropping her gaze to the baby as if the flattery was not meant for her.

… Okay… if you want to… she said.

He had a breath mint tucked between his tongue and cheek, and she could smell the mint.

Well… he said, I think the light is better over there. He pointed away from the crowded square toward a quiet side street where a few cars were parked. Let's go over there, it's better. He was handsome and confident.

She was a kind girl and always willing to please. She was flattered of the attention. The camera. She considered.

…Why not?…

The pigeons, regrouped behind him, took to the air again as one, startled by something not seen. The moon dangled.

…But …what is this thing embedded in his smooth voice?… something urgent, concealed… waiting…something…

She leveled her eyes square on him. Offered him a sweet smile. The baby stirred on her lap.

I don't think so, she said. But if you still want to take my picture, you're welcome to take it right here…

The man crouched and rested his chin on a fist. A statue with a camera. His eyes thirsty and not quite able to let her go. His huge shadow swallowed her compact figure while he shifted his weight from one foot to the other.

She sat motionless on the stone fountain bench and her hands clutched the baby. Her eyelids lowered and she detached and traveled inward until she disappeared. And she sat that way for a long time.

A warm blast of light tousled the air to shimmering. She looked up. He was gone.

He never took the picture.

*

She was glad to be back at her cabin in the still forest. The brook sang to her from under the trees. She unloaded her groceries and packages from the pickup and brought them in. When she had everything put away she sat in the rocker and nursed the baby for awhile. She rocked him gently until he had his fill. Then she put the baby in his pack and slipped her arms through the shoulder straps, and they went for a long walk in the tawny afternoon.

She hiked up an old logging road and in the mottled, concealing light among the deep ferns she came close to a doe with a spotted fawn. She was quiet and they were not alarmed. The doe was not afraid of her. She stood still and watched while the deer browsed. And after a while the doe and fawn faded into a blackberry thicket where their forms fractured beyond the screen of canes, and then the woods absorbed their buff light and they were gone.

*

I was in the bathroom shaving, and she was watching the evening news on the television.

O MY GOD... Then she called my name – COME QUICK!

She was very excited and I went to her with soap on my face.

That's him! she said, pointing to the wavy-haired man brooding on the television screen. That's the guy who wanted to take my picture that day in Eugene! Remember?... You were away working in Montana... years ago. I told you about it, remember? How many years ago was that? You probably don't remember. My god.

There are demons in this world, don't kid yourself. I don't know about the religious kind, but there are real ones. And victims though they may be themselves they are still demons, cunning and without compassion. Ted Bundy had a long run. A long, mad run. Why is it that the most awful of demons seek the most innocent among us as prey? The young women secretly discarded beneath a shamefully thin layer of forest dirt, never again to stir the waking morning with their loving industry. Random choices. Prey. What justice for them? Officious pronouncements? Righteous, enraged display? Justice is fanciful. A weighed gift from a blindfolded angel. We live in the illusion of choice while the ball rides a crazy slotted wheel and round and round it goes and where it stops nobody knows. Just the wheel, turning. Maybe, in the broader universe, the bigger picture, the one too big to see, there really is a plan and there really is such a thing as justice and all events do fit a perfect construct, the true purpose hidden for the time being and manifested, eventually. And maybe there is a heaven for the innocent, and maybe it will last longer than the projected and finite number of years the universe will expand until it eventually compresses back to a wad of solidity the size of a walnut. An eternal heaven where parting is no more and lasting forever and beyond judgment. Maybe it is expansive enough to hold the rest of us as well. All of us. All who have ever lived and ever will live and we will all be our true perfect selves, forever. I don't know. We can only hope while we stand naked and blind in the field awaiting the mowing. And sometimes we are thankful knowing we have perceived the path and radius of the swing and escaped by ducking the rampant steel blade of the scythe. The steady scythe. To stand another day. To stir the oatmeal while the baby awakens in yellow morning light and deer lower their heads at the soft corners of shadows. We are thankful.

A Boy

by Margaret-Dawn Thacker

When Ben was four years old he came home from pre-school one day and said, "Mason is going to have a little brother soon. Can we get one?"

Bruce and I laughed, told him he was handful enough, and went on with our plans for no more children.

This didn't deter Ben. He prayed out loud, every night, for a baby brother. He wished for one on his birthday cake candles and on shooting stars. Bruce and I would smile and shake our heads. Educating one child was expensive enough. We felt like we would be lucky if we could raise this one boy who rarely slept, walked in his sleep, asked questions, then didn't wait for answers, and couldn't learn where his personal space ended and that of someone else began.

Then, in December, before Ben turned six in March, the doctor surprised us with news of Ryan. We were stunned. Ben wasn't. He grinned, clapped his hands, and started making plans to share his room, his toys, and his wisdom with a brother.

"It may not be a boy," we cautioned.

Ben looked at us like we didn't have a clue as to how things worked. He never considered anything other than a brother and continued planning.

Ryan was born in August. My mother brought Ben to the hospital that afternoon after school. We have a picture of him holding tight to the bundle swaddled in blue. "I told them you were a boy," he said to his sleeping brother.

We were worried that he expected a baby brother to come out "playing age," but he didn't seem to mind that his sibling had some growing to do. He helped feed, rock, sing, and read to him. Ben drew the line at changing diapers. That was not his responsibility.

I missed the boys once and when I found them, Ben had taken Ryan outside in the stroller. He was sitting cross-legged in front of the baby, giving him the lowdown on the colors of fall leaves. Ryan listened intently.

Although learning disabilities kept Ben behind in school, he kept his brother ahead of peers by teaching him to tie his shoes, throw a two seam fast ball, and snag one of the back seats of the school bus where the cool kids sit. Ben struggled with multiplication tables, writing legibly, and sequencing activities, but he never struggled in his little brother's eyes. Ben only shined.

When Ryan started Kindergarten, he was named student of the week. He was allowed to bring anything he wanted from home for show and tell. His brother had begun Middle School in the building across the parking lot that same year. Ryan got permission for his brother to walk to the elementary school. Twelve year old Ben sat in front of his little brother's class in one of those tiny chairs while Ryan extolled all of Ben's virtues. Ben said he was embarrassed, but he still smiles when he talks about that day, saying, "Ryan was smart. I was a big kid and no one was going to bully him after they met me." Ben was right.

It's been hard on the two of them with Ben in college. Ryan keeps in touch by phone and social networking sites. They play Xbox live together on the weekend, long distance with headphones. I can hear Ben laughing through Ryan's headset.

Ben came home this weekend. Ryan sticks to his side. They wrestle, devour the contents of the refrigerator into all hours of the night, and laugh.

Ben met with his summer boss this afternoon before coming to town for dinner. He put our name on the reservation list and waited for us to arrive at the restaurant.

After paying for our meal Bruce and I walked outside to meet up with the boys. I pointed them out. They were walking across the parking lot toward Ben's car. Ben reached out and ruffled his brother's hair, grabbed him around the neck in a headlock and gave him a knuckle noogie. Ryan followed with a sharp elbow to Ben's ribs. They both laughed as they continued to push each other toward the car. As I watched the Explorer back out of the parking space, I was glad that the prayer of a small boy was answered sixteen years ago.

We Were All Swirling

by Gaboo

We were all swirling, wondering, "What will it be like? What will it be like?" So excited, none of us would dare an expectation.

Then the roll began.

A great impulse overwhelmed us and the truth boomed, "Okay, first up. You will be a Shetland pony, born in a barn, transported to a green pasture—you will sire 19 colts and die of an aneurysm while pulling a flower wagon. Takers?"

A thought beamed above us all and exclaimed, "Me! Me! Me!"

"Done." And fate was rested.

Next surged a different melody, "Okay, this one is a babe with bright eyes, unruly hair and a cleft palate. You will spend your formative years crawling on all manner of surfaces before wandering off a dock and drowning in a warm, inland lake. Anyone?"

Again a sprite rose to meet opportunity and cried out, "Me! Me! Pick Me!"

"Done." And the ribbon was tied.

An alluring smell of compulsion overcame me. I knew by my intuition that I must listen intently. The knowing boomed, "Okay, what this one holds in brevity is made up for through significance. You will be a small bird. You will experience the freedom of expansion from egg to outstretched wings. Your doting parents will adore you and you will fall from the nest, dying of exposure. In your passing you will inspire a writer, who will mark your tale, and in turn affect others in a circle of creation and contemplation. Let me hear you...?"

The compulsion filled me and my wants grew clearer, lighter. I rose to the occasion of choice and let my passion blossom, "Me! Me! Me! Oh do pick me!"

"Done," trumpeted the chorus and I was enveloped in sensation. Anatomical sensibilities flooded my understanding and I drifted into bliss—confused, anxious, and overwhelmed with wonder—settling into sleep as life took hold.

END

Dearest Reader,

Thank you for visiting and reading. This completes our final edition for Volume One. It was a year full of stories, but the path does not end. We are only travelers.

What inspires a writer? The reader. You are the writer's confidante, a companion on a quest sharing discoveries. Together, the writer and reader are astronauts of thought, voyagers critical to the mission, skirting the unknown, past archetypes and through swirling motivations, daring us all to know our world a little better. Peace, kindness, and much joy.

So you want to be an astronaut?
Books are good. Courses are good.
So's travel. So's a sidewalk cafe
Observe everything,
analyze this or that.
Words, phrases, rambling thoughts,
borderline insanity—
dreams—
forgetful of feeding times,
frustration with your pen,
the brain leaps
middle page, first page, no page,
pager goes off.
Share ideas, get ideas,
remove ideas,
ideas are fleas.
Catch a whisper, catch a thought,
a sidewalk cafe glance is caught.
Is she an interest for my plot?
Perhaps, she is an astronaut.

-Gaboo